P9-DBI-435

D0015037

D0015036

Lasers

Lasers

Other books in The Lucent Library of Science and Technology include:

Black Holes
Comets and Asteroids
Genetics
Global Warming

THE LUCENT LIBRARY OF SCIENCE AND TECHNOLOGY

Lasers

by Don Nardo

LUCENT BOOKS®

621.366
NAR

THOMSON

GALE

San Diego • Detroit • New York • San Francisco • Cleveland • New Haven, Conn. • Waterville, Maine • London • Munich

THOMSON

★ ™

GALE

On cover: A scientist focuses intently as he engages in laser research.

© 2003 by Lucent Books. Lucent Books is an imprint of The Gale Group, Inc.,
a division of Thomson Learning, Inc.

Lucent Books® and Thomson Learning™ are trademarks used herein under license.

For more information, contact
Lucent Books
27500 Drake Rd.
Farmington Hills, MI 48331-3535
Or you can visit our Internet site at http://www.gale.com

ALL RIGHTS RESERVED.
No part of this work covered by the copyright hereon may be reproduced or used in any form or by
any means—graphic, electronic, or mechanical, including photocopying, recording, taping, Web dis-
tribution or information storage retrieval systems—without the written permission of the publisher.

LIBRARY OF CONGRESS CATALOGING-IN-PUBLICATION DATA

Nardo, Don, 1947–
  Lasers / by Don Nardo.
    p. cm. — (The Lucent library of science and technology)
Summary: Discusses the scientific discovery and development of the use of high-intensity
light, called laser, and its use in our daily lives.
Includes bibliographical references and index.
  ISBN 1-59018-104-2
  1. Lasers—Juvenile literature. [1. Lasers.] I. Title. II. Series.
  TA1682 .N36 2003
  621.36'6—dc21
                                                              2001008206

Printed in the United States of America

Table of Contents

Foreword

"The world has changed far more in the past 100 years than in any other century in history. The reason is not political or economic, but technological—technologies that flowed directly from advances in basic science."

— Stephen Hawking, "A Brief History of Relativity," *Time*, 2000

The twentieth-century scientific and technological revolution that British physicist Stephen Hawking describes in the above quote has transformed virtually every aspect of human life at an unprecedented pace. Inventions unimaginable a century ago have not only become commonplace but are now considered necessities of daily life. As science historian James Burke writes, "We live surrounded by objects and systems that we take for granted, but which profoundly affect the way we behave, think, work, play, and in general conduct our lives."

For example, in just one hundred years, transportation systems have dramatically changed. In 1900 the first gasoline-powered motorcar had just been introduced, and only 144 miles of U.S. roads were hard-surfaced. Horse-drawn trolleys still filled the streets of American cities. The airplane had yet to be invented. Today 217 million vehicles speed along 4 million miles of U.S. roads. Humans have flown to the moon and commercial aircraft are capable of transporting passengers across the Atlantic Ocean in less than three hours.

The transformation of communications has been just as dramatic. In 1900 most Americans lived and worked on farms without electricity or mail delivery. Few people had ever heard a radio or spoken on a telephone. A hundred years later, 98 percent of American homes have telephones and televisions and more than 50 percent have personal computers. Some families even have more than one television and computer, and cell phones are now commonplace, even among the young. Data beamed from communication satellites routinely predict global weather conditions and fiber-optic cable, e-mail, and the Internet have made worldwide telecommunication instantaneous.

Perhaps the most striking measure of scientific and technological change can be seen in medicine and public health. At the beginning of the twentieth century, the average American life span was forty-seven years. By the end of the century the average life span was approaching eighty years, thanks to advances in medicine including the development of vaccines and antibiotics, the discovery of powerful diagnostic tools such as X rays, the life-saving technology of cardiac and neonatal care, and improvements in nutrition and the control of infectious disease.

Rapid change is likely to continue throughout the twenty-first century as science reveals more about physical and biological processes such as global warming, viral replication, and electrical conductivity, and as people apply that new knowledge to personal decisions and government policy. Already, for example, an international treaty calls for immediate reductions in industrial and automobile emissions in response to studies that show a potentially dangerous rise in global temperatures is caused by human activity. Taking an active role in determining the direction of future changes depends on education; people must understand the possible uses of scientific research and the effects of the technology that surrounds them.

The Lucent Books Library of Science and Technology profiles key innovations and discoveries that have transformed the modern world. Each title strives to make a complex scientific discovery, technology, or phenomenon understandable and relevant to the reader. Because scientific discovery is rarely straightforward, each title explains the dead ends, fortunate accidents, and basic scientific methods by which the research into the subject proceeded. And every book examines the practical applications of an invention, branch of science, or scientific principle in industry, public health, and personal life, as well as potential future uses and effects based on ongoing research. Fully documented quotations, annotated bibliographies that include both print and electronic sources, glossaries, indexes, and technical illustrations are among the supplemental features designed to point researchers to further exploration of the subject.

Introduction

Going Where No One Has Gone Before

O ne day in 1960 something happened that seemed almost magical to many people. Dr. Theodore Maiman put into operation a device that gave off a thin, bright red beam of light. This remarkable device was the world's first laser. It was called a ruby laser because Maiman passed ordinary light through a ruby to produce the laser light. Since that day hundreds of different kinds of lasers have been made, and thousands of practical uses have been found for these modern "supertools."

Until the invention of the laser, using powerful beams of light was an idea that appeared mainly in science fiction. The first important example was in H.G. Wells's classic *The War of the Worlds* (published in 1898). In the novel sinister Martians use a terrifying heat ray to attack the earth. Later, in the early comic strips, space heroes like Flash Gordon and Buck Rogers used deadly ray guns to fight their archenemies. Certainly, most people today are familiar with the exploits of Captains Kirk, Picard, Janeway, and Archer of the Starships *Enterprise* and *Voyager*. Fans of the *Star Trek* TV shows and movies know all about phasers and photon torpedoes, those fabulous, futuristic weapons of light. Equally famous are the light swords wielded by Luke Skywalker, Darth Vader, and other characters in the popular *Star Wars* films.

Of course all the devices mentioned above are destructive. This can be misleading, for science fiction is filled with examples of light being used for constructive purposes as well. For instance *Star Trek*'s characters use a small light source to perform operations, and they use beams of light to take apart thick metal walls, to repair broken circuits, and to generate holograms to create realistic virtual environments on the "holodeck."

Such advanced technology does not utilize normal everyday light, of course. It requires laser light, which is very different from ordinary natural light. The laser

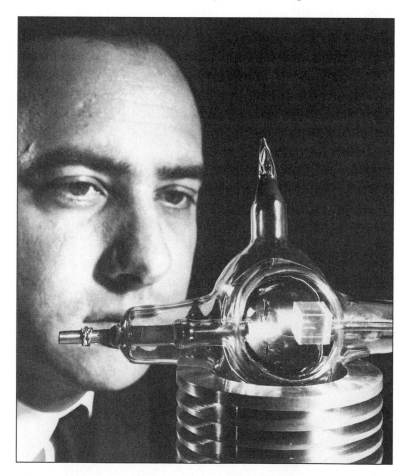

Dr. Theodore Maiman, creator of the first successful laser, examines an early version of the device. The cube inside is the ruby crystal that emitted the laser beam.

produces light that has been amplified, that is, made considerably brighter and more powerful. It took human beings, in their never ending search for new knowledge, to go beyond mere light, to invent the laser, and to take advantage of its marvelous properties. Just as Captains Kirk and Janeway go "where no one has gone before," scientists saw a light no one had seen before and put it to use for the good of all people.

Indeed, on that day in 1960 when the ruby laser began to glow, a new era began for humanity. The light no one had ever seen suddenly began to change science fiction into science fact. As lasers continue to advance rapidly and do more tasks in a wide range of scientific, medical, industrial, and commercial areas, it seems more and more likely that the society depicted in the world of *Star Trek* may be much closer than most people imagine.

Chapter 1

The Development of Lasers

A laser is a device that produces an unusually power-ful beam of light that does not exist on its own in nature. Today this light is used to perform thousands of useful tasks. A laser can give off a light beam that blasts through a thick metal wall or bores a hole in a diamond. Some lasers can measure things seen only under a microscope or even perform delicate eye operations. Every day, lasers are used in communications, factories, hospitals, and various entertainment media. In fact, lasers make our lives better and easier in so many ways that scientists have come to refer to these devices as the supertools of the modern age.

The invention of the laser was the result of many ideas and discoveries, each building upon the ones that came before it, going back more than a hundred years. Scientists did not purposely set out to invent the laser; in fact, no one seriously considered such a device until just a few years before the first laser was built. Most of the ideas that led to its invention were the results of attempts by scientists to learn more about light and how it behaves. As time went on, the idea that light might be made more powerful, or amplified, became more important to scientists. Only when a few researchers managed to put all these accumulated ideas together in a very special way did it occur to them that something like a laser could be built.

The Photophone and Early Theories of Light

The first important attempt to get light to perform a task that lasers perform today came in the year 1880. Noted American inventor Alexander Graham Bell performed an experiment that showed how light might be used to carry a person's voice from one location to another. To accomplish this, Bell used a device he called a photophone, which consisted of a thin mirror, a receiver that could detect light, some wires, and an earpiece. Bell placed the mirror so that sunlight reflected off of its surface and traveled more than one hundred feet to the receiver. When a person spoke near the delicate mirror, it vibrated slightly. This caused the sunlight being reflected into the receiver to vibrate, too. The receiver then changed the light vibrations into an electrical signal, which traveled through the wires to the earpiece.

A man demonstrates Alexander Graham Bell's photophone, a crude but ingenious attempt to make light transmit a human voice.

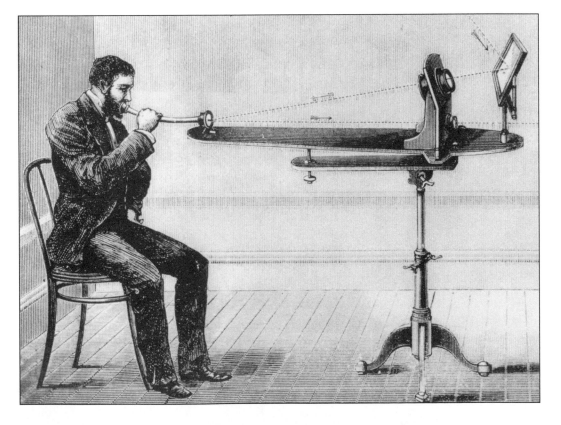

Unfortunately the photophone did not work very well. Bell's receiver was very crude compared to the ones used today. Also, the device relied on sunlight, which varies in brightness from hour to hour and from day to day. Obviously, on cloudy days or at night the device could not be used at all. Bell also had to contend with the fact that scientists at that time still did not know enough about light in order to use its power. What they did know was that light always travels at a set speed, which happens to be about 186,000 miles (300,000 kilometers) per second. This is so fast that a beam of light can race around the earth almost seven and a half times in a second.

But in order to use light as a tool it was not enough to know how fast light travels. People also needed to know what light is made of. Back in the 1600s English scientist Sir Isaac Newton had suggested that light was made up of tiny particles. This explanation became known as the particle theory of light. At about the same time, Dutch scientist Christian Huygens said that light might be composed of waves, similar to the ocean waves that roll onto a beach. Scientists dubbed this the wave theory of light.

Unfortunately, in Bell's day scientists still argued over which of these theories was correct. Through a mixture of hard work and genius, however, Bell managed to build a working photophone. The device itself operated on principles different from those that would later be used in the laser. Yet Bell had demonstrated that light might someday be used in communications. This idea prepared the way for the next step toward the discovery of the laser.

Einstein and Stimulated Light

In 1905 German scientist Albert Einstein announced his own theory about light, namely that it is made up of both particles *and* waves. Einstein claimed that the particles, called photons (from the Greek word for "light"), move along in wavelike patterns. Later, other scientists performed experiments that proved Einstein was right. Einstein himself then went on to predict some more startling things about light, first and foremost how photons are made. He agreed with some other scientists of his day about how light sources (like candles, light bulbs, or the sun) produce photons. The researchers thought that atoms (the tiny particles that make up all material in the universe) give off photons. Some form of energy—such as heat, electricity, or chemical energy— might "excite" an atom, or make it more energetic. It would then emit (give off) a photon. Afterward, the atom would go back to its normal, unexcited state. Because there are huge numbers of atoms, they give off equally large numbers of photons. A 100-watt light bulb gives off about 10 trillion photons every second.

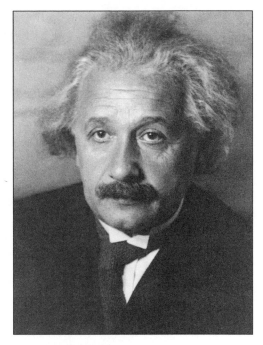

Physicist Albert Einstein suggested the concept of the stimulated, or amplified, emission of light.

In 1917 Einstein suggested that while an atom is excited it might be stimulated (coaxed) to produce a photon. If enough atoms could be excited and stimulated, a great number of photons might be produced. A beam of light made up of so many photons would be highly concentrated and therefore brighter and more powerful. Einstein called this process "stimulated emission of light." Because it can produce light that is boosted in power, or amplified, stimulated emission is the basic principle of laser operation.

Scientists had the basic information they needed to build a laserlike device as early as 1917. But no one actually attempted it. Researchers thought it would be too difficult and expensive; and they were right. The advanced machinery they needed did not exist at the time and would have to be developed piece by piece. The necessary research would take many years and cost a lot of money. Of course, such time and money would be worthwhile if the idea promised to be useful enough. But the vast majority of scientists at that time did not think the idea of amplifying light would lead to anything practical or useful. For this reason, the development of lasers occurred in a more roundabout way—through experiments with radar and microwaves.

Radar and Microwaves

During World War II (1939–1945) scientists worked hard at improving radar, a tracking device that had been invented a few years earlier. Radar sends out a beam of microwaves that bounces off nearby objects. Microwaves are similar to visible light, as both travel at 186,000 miles per second and are made up of particles that move

A naval technician tests radar equipment in August 1945. Experiments with radar led to technical advances that eventually produced the laser.

in waves. But unlike light, which people can see, microwaves are invisible to the eye. After a radar beam bounces off an object the reflected microwaves return and register on a screen. By studying the screen a radar operator can tell the general size and distance of the object. This is how soldiers located enemy airplanes during World War II.

As the war dragged on American military scientists tried to find ways of producing more powerful microwaves. Led by Dr. Charles Townes, these researchers found that microwave radiation does not work very well for radar because the waves are too easily absorbed by water vapor in the air; and as the beam travels farther more of it gets absorbed, so it gets too weak to do any good. But in a way, these experiments had not failed. They had made Townes very interested in learning more about microwaves, research that would eventually lead to the laser.

In 1947 Townes began teaching and doing research at Columbia University in New York City. He remembered what Einstein had said about the stimulated emission of visible light—that many atoms could be stimulated to produce many particles of light. Since microwaves are so similar to light, Townes reasoned that stimulation might also produce many microwave particles. If the microwaves could be produced by stimulation, perhaps enough of them could be built up to get an amplified beam. But what would be the purpose of such a beam? Townes was not sure it would have any practical uses, but he reasoned it would be an effective research tool to aid scientists in studying how atoms give off radiation.

The Maser—Precursor of the Laser

In 1951, while sitting on a park bench, Townes had a brilliant idea. He realized it might be possible to use molecules of ammonia to produce a powerful microwave beam. (A molecule consists of two or more atoms that are connected together.) Townes reasoned

Charles Townes (left) and James P. Gordon proudly display their maser, a device that greatly amplifies microwaves.

that when molecules of ammonia became excited (by heat, electricity, or chemical energy), they could be stimulated to emit microwaves of the type he was working with. He knew this process would be almost identical to the one Einstein described for stimulating visible light. The only difference was that Townes would be using microwaves instead of light. He calculated that if the ammonia molecules could be kept in an excited state long enough, they might be stimulated to produce more and more microwaves. Eventually, the waves would become concentrated and more powerful. In short, the microwaves would be amplified.

Townes decided to try to build a working model. He enlisted the aid of two other researchers, Herbert J. Zigler and James P. Gordon. Working diligently, by 1954 the three men had a working device that operated in the following way: First, some ammonia gas was heated until many of the molecules became excited and then were separated from the unexcited molecules. Next, the excited molecules flowed into a chamber called the resonant cavity (or resonator) where the stimulation of the molecules took place. As the excited ammonia molecules began to emit microwave particles, the particles began to bounce back and forth inside the chamber. When one of these particles came near an excited molecule, the molecule suddenly gave off its own particle. Thus the particles themselves stimulated the production of more particles. Soon the number of particles doubled, then doubled again and again until the microwaves in the chamber had become very powerful.

The entire process took only a tiny fraction of a second. Out of a hole in the resonator shot a strongly amplified beam of microwaves. The scientists called their invention a maser. The letters of this acronym stand for *m*icrowave *a*mplification by *s*timulated *e*missions of *r*adiation. The ammonia maser had only a few practical uses. First, because the ammonia molecules in the maser vibrated at a steady rate, the device could be used as a reliable timekeeping device. Second, because the maser was an amplifier, it could boost the weak microwave signals given off by distant stars, making it easier for astronomers to study such signals and learn more about stars.

Initial Laser Concepts and Designs

Townes and other researchers did not know it then, but the most important thing about the maser was that it set the stage for the development of the laser. All the right ingredients needed for the laser had been combined in the maser except for the most important one—light. In the mid-1950s, soon after the introduction of the maser, some researchers began talking about a device that would stimulate atoms to emit photons of light, exactly as Einstein had described. The photons would then be amplified to produce a powerful beam of light.

One researcher who wanted to learn how to amplify light was the father of the maser, Charles Townes. In September 1957 Townes drew a design for a device he called an "optical maser" (the term *laser* not yet having been coined). He then called another scientist, Arthur Schawlow, and the two men began drawing up more detailed plans for the optical maser. Townes and Schawlow were not the only ones work-

How a Maser Works

A maser amplifies, or increases, the number of photons that cause invisible electromagnetic waves known as microwaves. First, heated ammonia gas is pumped into the maser. There, "unexcited," or low-energy, molecules are drawn to the sides of the maser. Only "excited," or high-energy, ammonia molecules flow into the resonator, or vibrating chamber. In this chamber, the excited molecules begin to emit microwave photons. These photons bounce around in the resonator, striking the ammonia molecules so that they remain excited and produce more and more microwaves.

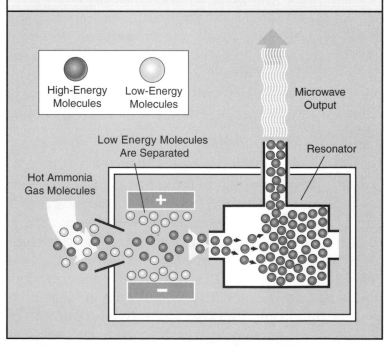

ing on the laser idea, however. Nikolai Basov and Aleksandr Prokhorov in the Soviet Union were also exploring the idea, and Gordon Gould, a graduate student at Columbia University, was thinking about developing his own light-amplifying device.

In November 1957, only two months after Townes had sketched the optical maser design, Gould wrote down in notebooks all his ideas for his own proposed invention. The first thing he wrote was a name for the device. He called it a laser, which stood for *l*ight *a*mplification by *s*timulated *e*mission of *r*adiation. Other researchers thought of this name on their own, but apparently Gould was the first to coin the term.

Hearing that Towne might also be working on lasers, Gould got worried. Naturally, he did not want someone else to get credit for what he considered to be his own invention. He showed his notes to a lawyer who specialized in patents. (When the government grants a person a patent for an invention, it recognizes that person as the original inventor. The person who holds the patent can also make a lot of money if the invention is successful.) Unfortunately for Gould, the lawyer did not understand the information in the notebooks and gave Gould the mistaken idea that he needed a working model of his invention in order to get a patent.

Gould was not sure what to do next, so he just waited. This turned out to be a mistake because in the meantime Townes and Schawlow had been hard at work. They applied for their own patent in the summer of 1958. They also wrote a paper explaining their ideas and had it published in a famous science magazine. Gould had not published a paper; and when he finally did apply for a patent, almost a year had elapsed since Townes and Schawlow had obtained their own patent. So no one believed Gould later when he claimed he had come up with the idea for lasers on his own.

Building the First Laser

By 1960 many scientists, including Townes and Schaw-low, Basov and Prokhorov, and Gould, had asked for laser patents. In addition, the paper published by Townes and Schawlow had caused widespread interest in lasers in the American scientific community. Researchers in labs around the country raced to be first to construct a working model. The first successful device appeared on July 7, 1960, built by a previously unknown researcher who had worked totally on his own—Theodore H. Maiman of the Hughes Aircraft Company in Malibu, California.

Maiman's laser was small (only a few inches long) and not very complicated. The core of the device consisted of an artificial ruby about one and a half inches long, so Maiman called his invention the "ruby laser." The ruby acted as the lasing medium, which is the substance that supplies the atoms or molecules to be stimulated. (In Townes's maser, the medium had been ammonia gas.)

Maiman knew that the atoms inside the ruby would need to be excited somehow. In the maser, the excitation method had been heat, but heating a ruby would only cause it to break. Searching for an alternate method, Maiman noted that light passes through a ruby, and he wondered if ordinary light itself could be used as the excitation device. Maiman rigged a powerful flash lamp so that it ran through a glass tube. The tube was bent into the shape of a coil and wound several times around the ruby. When the lamplight flashed, the photons excited the atoms in the ruby, and these excited atoms became stimulated and gave off their own photons.

Maiman had accomplished the first step in the lasing process. He had stimulated the atoms in the medium to produce photons. But to amplify the light, he needed to increase greatly the number of photons being produced. In the maser, amplification had occurred inside the resonant cavity where the particles bounced back and forth. In Maiman's laser the ruby itself acted as the resonator because it contained the excited atoms. However, there was nothing in the ruby for the photons to bounce off of. Furthermore, the ruby was nearly transparent. The photons created would just pass through and escape. Maiman had to figure out how to make the photons bounce back and forth and also how to keep them from escaping. He accomplished both of these goals in a very simple way: As the ruby was shaped like a cylinder (something like a long soup can but much smaller), Maiman coated each end of the ruby with silver. The ends then became mirrors pointing toward the center of the ruby. Because the mirrors faced each other, the photons bounced back and forth through the ruby over and over again.

The Ruby Laser

A ruby laser works much like a maser. But instead of microwaves, it produces an intense beam of visible light. This occurs when the molecules of an artificial ruby are "excited" by a flash of ordinary light from a flash tube, which surrounds the ruby. The "excited" ruby molecules begin to emit photons of visible light. The photons reflect off of mirrors located at both ends of the ruby. The reflected photons continue to excite more and more ruby molecules, thus producing more and more photons. This production of photons amplifies the light inside the ruby. The mirror on one end of the ruby is only a partial, or half-silvered, mirror, so some of the light passes through it. This light is the laser beam, or beam of amplified light.

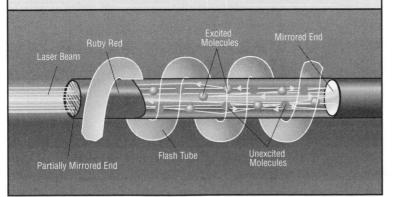

Laser Beam

Ruby Red

Excited Molecules

Mirrored End

Partially Mirrored End

Flash Tube

Unexcited Molecules

The next problem Maiman faced was how to allow his beam of amplified light to get by the mirrors and escape. His solution was to make the coating of silver on one end of the ruby very thin so that it became only a partial mirror, reflecting some photons back into the ruby while allowing others to escape. The ones that escaped became the actual laser beam. To Maiman's delight, the beam of strange deep red light shot out of the laser and registered on a nearby detector. As in the maser, the entire process happened extremely fast—in only a few millionths of a second.

A New Era Begins

Maiman immediately asked a scientific journal to publish the results of his experiment. But the editors of the journal did not realize the importance of the work and refused to publish the paper. So Maiman approached the editors of a British journal, *Nature,* and they agreed to publish his three-hundred-word article. Not surprisingly those few hundred words excited scientists all over the world, and dozens of labs began to build their own laser devices, initiating a new scientific era.

Researchers quickly realized that other materials besides the ruby could be used as laser mediums. The first gas laser used a mixture of helium and neon gases; and many other types of substances, including crystals, carbon dioxide gas, vaporized metal, and even colored dyes, became laser mediums. As more and different types of lasers were developed, scientists started thinking of tasks for lasers to perform. People in communications, industry, medical labs, and the military all rushed to find ways they might benefit from the new type of light. Astronomers wanted to use lasers to study the sun and stars; engineers wanted lasers to cut and weld metal parts; doctors saw potential for lasers in performing eye operations and burning away tumors; military leaders thought lasers might be developed into death rays to shoot down enemy planes; and so forth.

The laser also promised to benefit its inventor with a great deal of prestige and money. The problem was that several researchers had come up with the idea at about the same time. This made it difficult for the U.S. Patent Office to decide who the actual inventor was. As it turned out, Townes and Schawlow received patents for the basic laser principle, and Maiman received a patent for the ruby laser. However, because he had applied so late, Gould did not receive a patent; so he took the case to court. The legal battle dragged on for years.

Gould had even more to be upset about. In 1964 the famous Nobel Prize for physics was awarded to the men who had created the original designs for lasers. Three men shared the prize: Townes and the two Soviet scientists, Basov and Prokhorov. Again, Gould had been left out; and again, he refused to give up. Although he had to borrow large sums of money to continue the legal fight, it eventually paid off. In 1977 and 1979 Gould received patents for two small parts of the lasing process. Finally in 1988 the patent office granted him the major patent he had applied for back in 1959. And so, along with Townes, Schawlow, Maiman, Basov, and Prokhorov, Gould was at last recognized as one of the founding fathers of the laser.

Dr. Gordon Gould, who coined the term laser *in the 1950s, fought for recognition as one of the device's inventors.*

Chapter 2

Lasers in Science and Industry

Today scientists, lab technicians, engineers, and industrial technicians regularly utilize lasers to perform a wide range of important tasks. They measure distances, both short and long, with lasers, giving astronomers, geographers, and surveyors much more accurate figures than were available before the invention of these devices. They also use lasers to drill, weld, cut, and mark all sorts of materials; to study microscopic objects, including molecules; and even to fight crime.

Astronomy, Geography, and Surveying

One of the most important scientific uses for lasers is that of an advanced measuring tool. The potential of these devices to give precise figures for very long distances was shown in 1969 when the *Apollo 11* astronauts became the first men ever to walk on the moon. Before blasting off on their return flight they left behind a bizarre-looking mirror. A short time later scientists on Earth claimed that the strange mirror had revealed to them the distance from Earth to the moon, a figure that was accurate to within the length of a person's finger. This moon mirror was neither mysterious nor magical, though it would have seemed so to many people only a few years before. In reality, National Aeronautics and Space Administration (NASA) scientists had instructed the astronauts on exactly how to position the mirror as part of a plan to measure the Earth-to-moon distance with a laser beam.

Before lasers existed, scientists already had a fairly good idea of how far away the moon is. But "fairly good" is not good enough in science. Scientists want their measurements to be as exact as possible, and bouncing a laser beam off the mirror promised to give

U.S. astronaut Buzz Aldrin stands on the moon's surface. There, the astronauts placed a special mirror designed to reflect back a laser beam sent from Earth.

them more accurate figures than ever before. The experiment used the simple formula

$$r \times t = D$$
(rate multiplied by time equals Distance)

The scientists already knew the speed of light, so they knew what the rate of travel was. When the beam bounced off the mirror, it returned to Earth and registered on special sensors. These recorded how long the beam took to make a round trip, and scientists then knew the time factor in the equation. After some simple multiplication, they finally had the most accurate measurement of the Earth-to-moon distance possible. Knowing this has enabled them to learn much about the relationship between Earth and its natural satellite. For instance, researchers have repeated this laser-mirror experiment every year since 1969. They have found that the moon is moving away from Earth at a rate of about one and a half inches (four centimeters) a year.

Measuring distance by means of lasers and mirrors works just as well on Earth as it does in space. Every day, surveyors use lasers to measure the distances between houses, roads, and mountains. A device called a range finder utilizes the same principle as the moon mirror; a surveyor aims a laser beam at a reflective target and the beam bounces back to the range finder, which records the time of the round-trip and uses this figure to calculate the exact distance to the target. This method is more accurate and also much faster than older surveying methods, which required many calculations with poles and telescopes that had to be lined up with one another. Erecting skyscrapers, excavating tunnels and canals, laying pipelines, drilling wells, leveling farmland (making it flatter and easier to exploit) are only a few of the many other projects made easier by precise laser measurements. Such measurements also have led to more exact and reliable maps; using lasers, mapmakers have now charted almost every square mile of Earth's surface.

Measuring Distances with Lasers

Lasers can measure enormous distances with great accuracy. A laser beam travels at a constant speed (the speed of light). The time it takes a laser beam to travel from its source, reflect off an object, and return to the source, will indicate the exact distance between the source and the object.

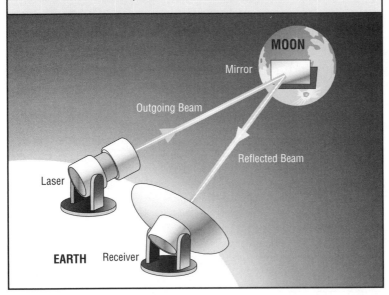

Laser Toolbox Technology

Such precise measurement is just one of several jobs that, before the advent of lasers, were associated with what engineers and others call "toolbox" technology. Every toolbox has its yardstick, ruler, or tape measure. It also has a drill to bore holes and a hacksaw to cut metal. Larger toolboxes include welding equipment to join pieces of metal together. Just as lasers have come to replace the yardstick in measuring, they also have replaced the drill, the saw, and the welder. The era of the toolbox laser has arrived.

Lasers perform some toolbox jobs better and faster because of some unusual properties of laser light itself. In the first place, laser light is extremely bright, so bright that laser operators always wear protective glasses. The light is so intense because its energy is very concentrated; there are a great number of photons in a relatively small beam.

Laser light is also highly directional, or collimated. This means that all the photons travel in the same direction. They tend to stay together rather than spread apart as the photons in ordinary light do. The farther a beam of ordinary light travels, the more it spreads out and gets dimmer. On the other hand, collimated laser light can travel a great distance without losing very much of its energy and brightness. Ordinary light could never have made it to the moon mirror and back, whereas laser light did quite easily.

Properties of Laser Light

The photons of laser light are collimated. In other words, they all travel from the laser in the same direction. Laser light is also coherent, meaning that all the waves in a laser beam have the same wave pattern. These properties make laser light more intense than ordinary light and allow it to travel long distances. Ordinary light waves scatter in all directions from their source. Also, an ordinary beam of light is incoherent, meaning that it contains waves of many different patterns, which tend to interfere with one another.

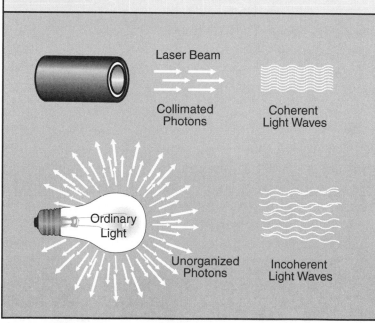

Laser Beam

Collimated Photons

Coherent Light Waves

Ordinary Light

Unorganized Photons

Incoherent Light Waves

There is one more important quality of laser light. It is coherent, or very organized. This means that the light waves are lined up with each other and moving along in step, almost like a regiment of soldiers marching in a parade. By contrast, ordinary light is incoherent. Its waves become mixed up as they move along, like the crowd of people watching the parade. So, the laser light is special. It is concentrated, directional, and organized.

These three qualities combine to make the laser an extremely powerful and useful tool in materials processing, the industrial manipulation of metals, plastics, wood, ceramics, cloth, and other materials for making a wide range of products. Breck Hitz, an expert on industrial lasers, elaborates:

> Lasers are used to cut, drill, weld, heat-treat, and otherwise alter both metals and nonmetals. Lasers can drill tiny holes in turbine blades more quickly and less expensively than mechanical drills. Lasers have several advantages over conventional techniques of cutting materials. For one thing, unlike saw blades or knife blades, lasers never get dull. For another, lasers make cuts with better edge quality than most mechanical cutters. The edges of metal parts cut by a laser rarely need to be filed or polished because the laser makes such a clean cut.[1]

Drilling and Burning Holes with Light

A laser beam excels as an industrial drill because it can be focused into a tiny bright point. Of course, ordinary light can be focused in a similar way. For instance, a magnifying glass held up to the sun will focus the sun's rays into a tiny, very bright point, a point that is also hot enough to burn a leaf or ignite a piece of paper.

Now consider collimated laser light, which is hundreds of times more directional than ordinary light. It can be focused to produce a beam of light, much hotter than the surface of the sun, that can cut cleanly through a thick metal bar in a few millionths of a second.

One of the more important uses of the laser drill in industry is in the production of copper wire. The wire is formed by forcing copper metal into a small round hole that a laser has drilled into a diamond. The hard diamond acts like a mold, and the much softer copper squeezes out the other end in the form of wire. The old method of drilling holes in industrial diamonds was very time-consuming and expensive. Since the only naturally occurring material hard enough to cut through a diamond is another diamond, workers had to use diamond drills. But diamonds are expensive. Furthermore, the drilling process took several hours, so a worker could drill only two or three holes in a work-day. In contrast, a laser beam drills holes in diamonds at the speed of light. One worker using one laser can bore hundreds or even thousands of holes in a single hour. And the same method is used for drilling holes in other gems that are used as moving parts in watches.

These tiny diamond dies used in telephone lines have been drilled with laser beams. Such small holes could not be cut in diamonds without lasers.

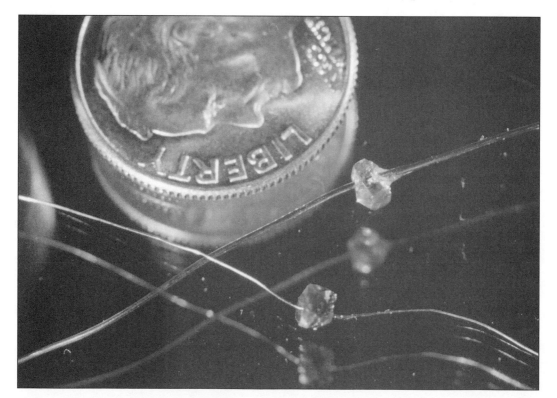

Though it might seem surprising, lasers are also effective in boring holes in very soft materials. Some of these materials are easily stretched or torn by ordinary methods. An excellent example is the common baby bottle nipple. A laser beam burns a perfectly round hole in the top of the nipple without disturbing any of the surrounding rubber. Similarly, lasers are used to drill tiny holes in the soft plastic valves of spray cans (such as those of hair spray or glass cleaner). One such laser can punch over a thousand valve holes in one minute.

Welding and Cutting with Lasers

Another industrial application of lasers is welding. The advantage of the laser over normal welding methods is similar to its advantage in other industrial areas. The laser is hotter, faster, more accurate, and also safer because the welder does not have to go near the hot metal.

Laser welding works on both large and small scales. On the large scale, the U.S. Navy uses lasers to weld together huge metal parts in shipbuilding. Experts estimate that millions of dollars are saved in the welding process and millions more in reduced need for later repairs. Such common items as automobile spark plugs, portable batteries, and metal braces for the teeth are also routinely welded by laser beams.

On a smaller scale, lasers weld the parts for tiny electrical circuits used in computers, calculators, and miniature television sets. In the past, welding these small parts was accomplished by soldering—melting a metallic substance called solder around them to ensure a proper electrical connection. But soldering tools cannot be made small enough to weld the very tiny electrical parts now being produced; and manipulating the smallest available soldering tools is very painstaking work, produces uneven results, and can damage the delicate parts. By contrast, such tiny welds, some of them even microscopic, are easily made by the hot, razor-thin beam of a carbon dioxide laser.

In industry the opposite of welding is cutting, another essential process for making all manner of products.

A technician uses a laser to cut holes in carbon steel, one of the hardest of all artificial substances.

Every good toolbox has a hacksaw and a pair of scissors; the saw to cut metal, the scissors to cut cloth. The toolbox laser can do the jobs of both. Making saw blades themselves is an excellent example of using lasers to cut metal. The old methods of producing saw blades involved many steps, each of which required a person to handle the blades with his or her hands; not surprisingly, injuries were common. In contrast, a laser cuts the blade out of the sheet metal in only one step. Only the beam touches the metal, so as long as the operator is wearing protective glasses there is no chance for injury. In addition, reflective substances like glass can be cut by a laser if their surfaces are first coated with a dark substance. That way the laser light is absorbed rather than reflected.

An example of the use of "laser scissors" is to cut patterns for clothes. A laser cloth-cutting system was designed by Hughes Aircraft, the company that employed Theodore Maiman, the inventor of the ruby laser. The system works in the following way: Pieces of cloth are laid out on a large table while the patterns are entered into a computer, which decides the best way to trace them out on the cloth. Next, the computer directs the laser beam to cut out the traced patterns very precisely. Cloth for hundreds of suits can be cut in an hour, and as an added advantage the heat of the beam keeps the edges of the cloth from fraying.

Such laser scissors can be made to work on a microscopic level as well, not only in industry but also in biological research. Scientists who study and attempt to manipulate plant or animal cells can use a laser beam to make tiny alterations—in a sense performing microsurgery—on such cells. Recent experiments show that the use of lasers also can eliminate a serious obstacle to such microscopic manipulation; namely, the difficulty of holding a cell in place while working on it. To accomplish this task laser scissors are often accompanied by "laser tweezers," as explained by University of California scholar Michael Berns:

> That light can heat or burn, measure or calibrate makes sense. But the idea of light creating a force that can hold and move an object may seem as fanciful as a Star Trek tractor beam. Still, light has momentum [a forward-pushing force] that can be imparted to a target. The resultant [very small] forces fall far below our sensory awareness when, for example, the sun's light falls on and imperceptibly pushes against us. But these forces can be large enough to influence biological processes at the subcellular level, where the masses of the objects are [extremely tiny]. . . . When the geometry

of the arrangement of light beams and target is correct, the momentum imparted to the target pulls the target in the direction of the . . . laser beam, and the beam can thus hold the target in place. By moving the beam, the laser operator can pull the target from place to place.[2]

Fighting Crime with Lasers

The toolbox laser can even be used, along with other scientific tools such as DNA testing, to fight crime. A laser beam can scan a computerized record of millions of criminals' fingerprints, for instance, and in a few seconds pick out one that matches a print found at a crime scene. Laser beams can also detect extremely minute and very old traces of perspiration and other human body secretions. In the 1990s the FBI investigated a man they believed to be a former German Nazi in World War II. He denied the charge. But then the FBI obtained a postcard written by the Nazi in 1942, and a laser was able to find traces of body oils on the card; the oils were identical to those of the suspect, who was found guilty and imprisoned.

In another example of lasers acting as detectives, some people are recovering stolen gems thanks to a system called laser identification. An ID marking is carved into the gem by a laser that creates a thin and accurate beam. This beam, which is so tiny it can cleanly drill more than two hundred holes in the head of a pin, carves or etches microscopic numbers, words, people's names and addresses, or entire messages on any material, no matter how smooth or hard. This includes precious gems like emeralds and diamonds. The result is an ID marking so tiny that no one, including a thief, can detect it with the naked eye. Many other valuable items are now marked in this manner by laser beams.

Almost every day several new uses are found for toolbox lasers. The devices are still rather expensive, so

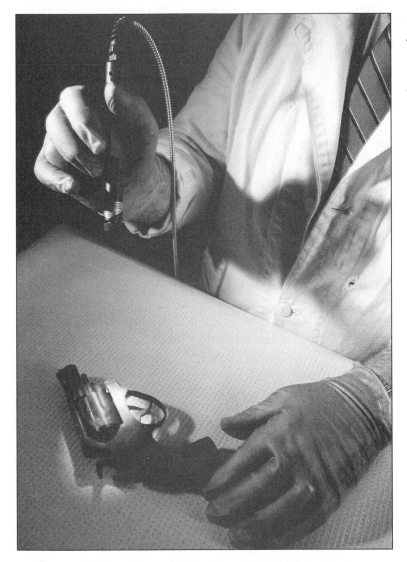

In addition to marking guns with tiny ID numbers, lasers can be used to detect finger-prints on handguns and other weapons.

they are not yet normally found in home toolboxes. But this situation will surely change. As laser research continues, ways will be found to produce these tools more simply and cheaply. In the near future a laser hanging above the basement workbench may become a common sight.

Chapter 3

Lasers in Communication and Marketing

Just as a person who can read and write is said to be literate, a laser that can read and write can also be thought of as literate. Such a feat is possible because of the joining together of the laser and another modern supertool—the computer. Computers are able to process information thousands of times faster than human beings. For instance, hundreds of years ago when a scientist needed to solve a complicated math problem, he or she had to do all the adding and multiplying by hand. A single problem might take as long as three months to solve. Today's supercomputers can give the answer to the very same problem in only three seconds. What is more, computers allow all kinds of marketing and communications tasks—from supermarket scanning to office copying to sending documents and music files across the country—to be accomplished much quicker and easier than by traditional means.

Both scientists and consumers used to have one major problem with computers, however. To feed new information into the computer the operator had to type the words on a keyboard; and people can only type so fast. There was a similar problem at the other end of the computing process. In order for the information that came out of the computer to be readable, the computer itself had to use a keyboard. A computer can type much faster than a person, but the typing still took a considerable amount of time. So even though a computer could process information quickly, a lot of time was wasted during the input and output stages. The advent of laser scanning technology has greatly alleviated this problem; and the world is in the midst of a veritable revolution in laser-computer literacy that is changing the face of both businesses and homes.

Laser Scanners and Printers

A laser scanner is a sophisticated device; but its basic principle is fairly simple. On the input end, a tiny laser beam scans across a page of text, a bar code, a photograph, or another image to be scanned. As it moves, the beam reflects back into a sensor that records the alternating patterns of white and black or of various colors.

A man has his face scanned by a laser beam (left). A video camera detects the beam and feeds it into a computer, which creates a profile for use in facial recognition systems.

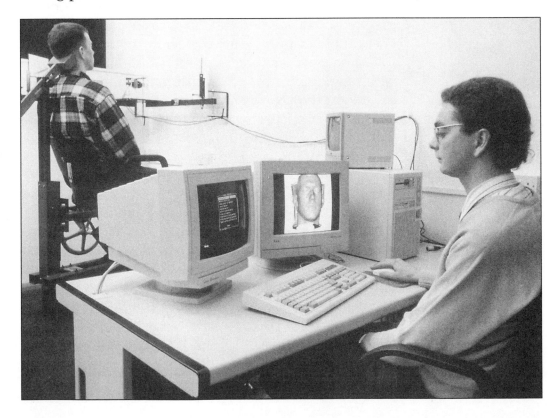

A computer has been preprogrammed to recognize these patterns and translates them into electrical impulses.

On the output end, when the computer has information ready to be printed out, the laser once more speeds up the process. The computer "orders" the laser beam to modulate its intensity, that is, to get brighter, then dimmer, then brighter, and so forth, as needed. The modulated beam is now scanned across a light-sensitive material, usually a TV screen or sheet of paper, as in the case of a laser printer. The beam literally "writes" the information on the material (and/or stores it in the computer's memory). A laser printer also prints out information gathered by a computer from online web pages.

This and similar laser-computer systems are used every day to make money transactions. For instance, almost everyone receives monthly bills (for electricity, gas, and credit cards) that have been printed with a laser, and the vast majority of payroll checks are printed the same way. Such laser printers also supply people with news and information. All major and even most small local newspapers now use lasers to make printing plates. The laser beam etches the information on the light-sensitive plate in roughly the same way it writes on a screen or on paper.

Lasers in the Supermarket

Laser scanning technology has helped make many traditional jobs easier and less boring. An excellent example is the kind seen in supermarkets. These devices, first seen in a few stores in the 1970s and now virtually universal in American supermarkets, read the bar code (Universal Product Code, or UPC) that appears on all food packages in the United States. The Supermarket Institute in Washington, D.C., introduced the bar code in 1973. With the scanner and bar code, the checkout clerk no longer needs to press cash register buttons for every item. This not only makes the clerk's job easier

The Bar Code Laser Scanner

A supermarket bar code laser works in the following manner: A twelve-ounce box of Kellogg's Corn Flakes carries a bar code whose stripes stand for the numbers 381100. When the box is pulled across the scanner the laser beam reads these stripes and relays the message to the computer memory bank. The computer knows (because it has been programmed to know) that these particular stripes stand for product number 381100. The computer also knows that product 381100 is Kellogg's Corn Flakes, twelve-ounce size. (Smaller or larger boxes of the same product have similar but unique bar codes.) After identifying the product the computer looks up the price, which has also been programmed in. Next, the name of the product and the price appear on the monitor above the cash register. The total elapsed time from scanning to readout on the screen is a mere fraction of a second. When all the customer's products have been scanned, the machine adds up all the prices and the total for the transaction appears on the screen.

but also reduces the chance for errors. A beam of light is much less likely to make a mistake than a person who is distracted, nervous, or just plain tired. In addition, the customer gets through the line and out of the store more quickly than before.

Another advantage of the bar code system is that it helps the supermarket with inventory. For instance, suppose there are one hundred boxes of corn flakes on the shelves when the store opens. Each time one of these boxes is sold, the computer records it. At the end of the day, the store manager checks the records, and if the computer indicates that eighty-seven boxes of flakes sold that day, the manager knows the supply is low and reorders immediately. This obviously saves a great deal of time in walking up and down store aisles and counting cans and boxes.

Supermarket laser scanners most often use a helium-neon gas laser that emits a red beam. Very dependable, it is also one of the least expensive types of laser. This is important because supermarket chains buy hundreds, sometimes even thousands, of the devices and could not afford the more expensive versions. The beam is powerful enough to read the bar codes but not so bright that it will hurt someone's eyes if he or she accidentally looks at it.

Office Uses of Lasers

Bar codes, which are also used on magazines, books, greeting cards, and most other consumer goods, are not the only things laser beams can read. Facsimile, or fax, machines use laser beams to read documents, which are then transmitted from one office or home to another. These locations can be thousands of miles apart, their only requirement being that each end have a fax machine.

Many fax machines employ a helium-neon laser not unlike the type used in supermarkets. The laser beam in the first office scans the page that will be sent (called the original document). The images contained in the reflected beam are converted into electrical energy and transmitted by wires or antennas to the machine in the second office. There the energy is reconverted into light images, and a laser burns these images onto a light-sensitive metal drum. Finally, the drum transfers the information onto paper, and the process is complete. The whole procedure takes only about two minutes or less, a fraction of the time taken by old-fashioned hand delivery.

Laser printers, which are in practically every office as well as in the majority of private homes, operate similarly to laser fax machines. The printers also use laser beams to burn images into light-sensitive materials. Such printers have revolutionized the printing and copying market in the past three decades because they produce many copies quickly; make unusually clear, clean copies; and allow a wide range of printing jobs to be performed in a office or home, including making flyers, wedding announcements, reports, and even entire books, as well as printing computerized addresses on envelopes.

The Light That Talks

One quality of laser light that makes it ideal for these and other kinds of information-exchange and communication is that it can carry a great deal of information.

The amount of information light can carry depends on its frequency. Imagine going to the beach two days in a row. On the first day the ocean waves are long and lazy, their crests averaging about fifty feet apart. On the second day the situation is much different, with waves that are now much shorter and more energetic, their crests only about five feet apart. Obviously there are more waves (ten times more to be exact) breaking per minute on the second day than on the first. Because the waves on day two are more frequent, they are said to have a higher frequency.

Waves of the different types of radiation (radio, microwaves, or light, for example) behave somewhat like the ocean waves. The lower frequency radiation waves are long and lazy. The higher frequency waves are short and energetic. The important point here for communications is that the higher the frequency, the more information can be carried. Consider that the telephone transmits the human voice at a frequency of about three thousand waves, or cycles, per second. That sounds like a large number of waves until it is compared to a television signal. Television transmits at a frequency of about 108 million cycles per second. Obviously a lot more information can be carried by a television signal than by a telephone signal. In fact, that is why the telephone can only transmit a voice, whereas television can broadcast both voice and picture.

But even the frequency of television signals is small compared to beams of light. Visible light frequencies range between 400 trillion and 800 trillion cycles per second. That means that light has the capacity to carry more than a million times as much information as television. In communications, the amount of information exchanged is the most important factor. It is no wonder then that the laser, which uses light to transmit information, has been so revolutionary.

Sending Signals Through Air and Cables

Such laser-based communications work in two basic ways. One way involves transmission directly through

Wave Frequency

Electromagnetic waves occur in a variety of frequencies, or waves (cycles), per second. The more waves per second, the higher the frequency, and the more information the waves can carry. The frequency of TV signals, for example, is 108 million cycles per second. Visible light has about 10 million times that many. Ultraviolet light, detectable by X-ray cameras, has a frequency ten times higher than visible light.

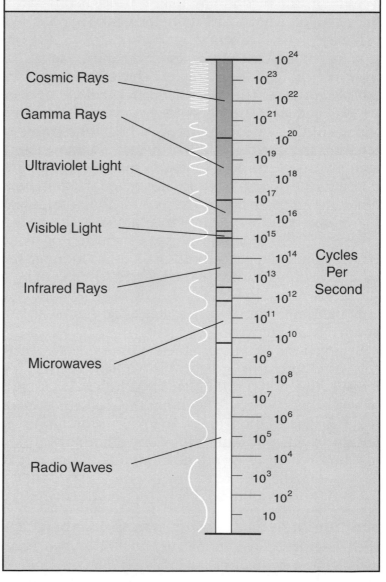

Cosmic Rays

Gamma Rays

Ultraviolet Light

Visible Light

Infrared Rays

Microwaves

Radio Waves

10^{24}
10^{23}
10^{22}
10^{21}
10^{20}
10^{19}
10^{18}
10^{17}
10^{16}
10^{15}
10^{14}
10^{13}
10^{12}
10^{11}
10^{10}
10^{9}
10^{8}
10^{7}
10^{6}
10^{5}
10^{4}
10^{3}
10^{2}
10

Cycles
Per
Second

the atmosphere (or through space). The same principle that allowed the direct transmission of a laser beam to a mirror on the moon could be used to communicate with astronauts on a moon base, for example. In this case the beam would carry stores of information and would not bounce back to Earth. A receiver in the base would pick up the beam and a computer would decode it.

The same procedure is already in common use in many earthbound cities. Several businesses have set up systems to flash laser beams from building to building. Some park services also use the system to communicate with rangers stationed at bases on remote mountains, where installing telephone lines could be too expensive. The ranger has a radio, of course; but if a large amount of information must be sent, the laser is a better choice. A fellow ranger at the main headquarters sends a communications beam to a receiver at the mountain base. A small computer in the base decodes the beam.

Unfortunately, light does not travel well through the atmosphere. The individual molecules of air tend to absorb some of the photons as they travel along, so the farther the light goes the dimmer it gets. As a result, scientists have learned to bypass the atmosphere by sending laser light through enclosed cables, the basis of the science of fiber optics.

A crude version of fiber optics appeared in 1934 when an inventor named Norman R. French patented an idea for a device called the "light pipe." French proposed taking a hollow pipe and lining it with a reflective material. If someone shined a light into the pipe, the rays might bounce off the inner surface and keep going through the tube.

French did not intend to send information with his device but rather to find a way to carry illumination from one room to another. But scientists in the 1960s believed that the light-pipe idea could be adapted to the field of laser communications. They quickly realized that the pipe they needed could not actually be hollow because then it would still contain air, and the air would absorb the light as it does in the atmosphere. Also, the signal would lose some of its power because small amounts would be absorbed by the lining itself. Another problem was that light travels in straight lines and the pipe would have to curve now and then to avoid obstacles (especially since it would be placed underground). They had to find a way to keep the curves from blocking the beam.

A major breakthrough came in 1966 when two British researchers, Charles Kao and George Hockham, suggested that thin glass fibers might be able to transmit light over short distances. Other scientists quickly picked up the idea, and in 1970 Robert Maurer of the Corning Glass Works in Corning, New York, constructed the first long-distance optical fiber. The science of fiber optics was born.

The fiber-optic system uses glass fibers only a fraction of an inch in diameter. The fibers, which make up the core, are stuffed inside a small cable that is lined with a material known as the cladding. This is an extremely reflective type of glass that makes most of the stray photons bounce back into the core. The cladding eliminates the problem of the beam not being able to move around curves; as long as the curves are not too sharp, the beam hits the cladding at an angle, then moves on. Such cables now regularly carry phone conversations, e-mail and the Internet, television signals, and other kinds of information. According to the National Academy of Engineers:

> By the end of 1998, there were more than 215 million kilometers [133 million miles] of [laser] optical fiber installed for communications worldwide. The optical fibers transmit light pulses up to 13,000 miles, and are handling data rates that are doubling each year. Today, optical fibers are the best conduit for delivering an array of interactive services, using combinations of voice, data, and video. [3]

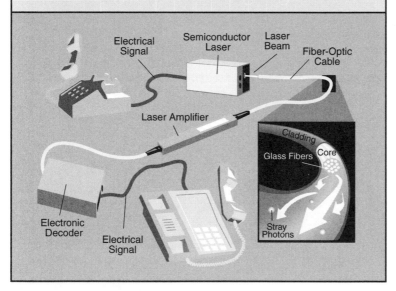

Lasers and Fiber-Optic Communication

Optical fibers are thin strands of glass through which a laser beam can travel for several miles. Since a laser sends signals on light waves, a single optical fiber can carry as much information as hundreds of heavy copper wires, which carry electrical signals. When electrical signals travel through copper wires, they are quickly weakened. Devices called repeaters are needed about every mile to strengthen the electrical signal. In a fiber-optic system, laser amplifiers are needed only every six or seven miles to strengthen the light signal.

Electrical Signal · Semiconductor Laser · Laser Beam · Fiber-Optic Cable · Laser Amplifier · Cladding · Glass Fibers · Core · Electronic Decoder · Electrical Signal · Stray Photons

A Fiber-Optic Society

Since a laser beam can carry high-quality television signals, most pay-television providers now install cable TV lines that use laser fiber optics. (An alternative is satellite dishes, which collect television signals bounced off of satellites.) In some towns and regions, companies are also connecting groups of homes and/or businesses to each other in small networks. Utilizing such a network, a person can broadcast a daily exercise class from his or her living room and ten, twenty, or more subscribers (those paying for the service) can tune in and participate within the comfort of their own homes or offices.

Advantages of Fiber-Optic Cables

One of the advantages of laser fiber optics is that several fibers can be wrapped inside one cable. This means that each cable contains many laser beams, each carrying billions of bits of information. This makes the optical system clearly superior to earlier systems. For instance, the old-style telephone cable used wires to transmit conversations. Obviously, to carry many conversations there had to be many wires in a single cable, which made the cable quite thick, heavy, and difficult to install. Also, since the metal wires had to be packed so closely together the separate signals sometimes interfered with each other and produced electrical noise. By contrast, the optical telephone system uses a much thinner, lighter cable that is easier to install. Beams of light do not interfere with each other, so there is no noise in the system. A large conventional telephone cable could carry as many as a few thousand conversations at one time. By contrast, fiber-optic cables now exist that can carry millions of conversations at one time.

A fiber-optic cable (right) containing 144 tiny glass fibers is compared with a cross section of a conventional copper cable.

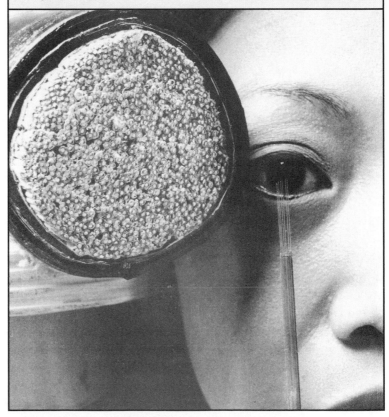

Some local areas of the United States, Japan, and a few other industrialized nations are presently experimenting with fiber-optic systems that connect individual homes to libraries and other storehouses of information. When a person asks a librarian to enter a book, magazine article, or even a movie into the library computer, the local cable carries the requested information to a monitor screen in the person's home. As demand increases, such systems will become more widespread and eventually as commonplace as the telephone.

The choice of the laser for these future communications systems is inevitable because laser light can carry vast amounts of information. It has been estimated that more than 100 million television channels might be transmitted using the frequencies in the spectrum of visible light. Even if only one-tenth of 1 percent of this total is ever used, that is still one hundred thousand channels. Only laser light will be able to carry that much information and thereby transform the way human beings communicate.

Chapter 4

Military Applications of Lasers

The U.S. military became interested in lasers even before the first lasers had actually been built. When military leaders heard that the new device might produce very hot beams of light, they immediately dreamed of developing beam weapons. They hoped these weapons would do many things that ray guns had done in science fiction stories, including blasting holes through enemy soldiers and tanks or even shooting down planes and satellites.

Much of the military's early exposure to the laser idea came from Gordon Gould, the laser pioneer who had so much difficulty getting recognition for his work. Even though he was having trouble getting a patent, he continued to work on lasers; and when he left Columbia University in 1959 he went to work for Technical Research Group (TRG), a company in Syosset, New York, that did research on radar, missiles, and other military projects. Gould got TRG very interested in lasers. TRG then asked the U.S. Department of Defense for three hundred thousand dollars to do research on laser weapons. The military was so fascinated by the idea of beam weapons that it gave the company almost a million dollars, more than three times the amount that had been requested.

A few months later when Maiman built the first ruby laser, his own company, Hughes Aircraft, began working on laser weapons. Soon, various branches of the military—army, navy, and air force—gave money to several other companies to develop such weapons. Between 1962 and 1968 the army alone spent almost $9 million on laser research.

Star Trek's *Mr. Spock brandishes a phaser pistol, a formidable fictional weapon. Modern weapons designers began trying to exploit the laser's potential for warfare.*

But could such death rays actually be built? The answer, at least at that time, was no. Scientists found that lasers did indeed produce very concentrated beams of light. But building the kinds of weapons the military wanted turned out to be much more difficult than everyone had figured. "So far lasers have been found to make poor weapons," says Breck Hitz, "and many scientists believe that engineering complexities and the laws of physics may prevent them from ever being particularly useful for this purpose."[4] Nevertheless some researchers are more optimistic about the potential of laser weapons, and intensive research and development continues. At the same time, the laser continues to prove highly applicable and useful in other battlefield roles such as range finding and designating targets.

A Lopsided Energy Ratio

The main difficulty faced by scientists attempting to build laser-beam weapons has been a lopsided ratio between the amount of energy needed to power the weapon and the amount the weapon produces. In the case of handheld ray guns, for example, too much energy is required for devices so small. To produce enough power

Electrically Powered Laser Weapons

At present most experiments with laser-beam weapons rely on chemical mediums—such as oxygen-iodine—to produce the energy to power the laser. But the U.S. Air Force and other groups are working on the idea of carrying special generators on attack aircraft. Such generators would produce electrically powered laser weapons that utilize fiber-optic technology. Fiber optics would allow the generators to be built much smaller than the equipment needed to produce chemically powered lasers; so such a weapons system would easily fit in a small fighter plane (as opposed to a 747 freighter, which is slower and less versatile). There would also be a nearly unlimited supply of "shots" as the generators constantly produce new energy. Such weapons could be positioned on a plane's wings, ready to fire at any oncoming missiles.

such guns would have to be so huge no one could carry them. Also, the guns themselves would get very hot, hot enough to cause serious burns on the hands of the people holding them (unless they wore thick protective gloves, which would hinder operation of the weapon). Over the years, researchers repeatedly found that, for the time and money required to build them, ordinary rifles would be more effective handheld weapons than lasers.

For a long time, lasers that could shoot down planes or satellites seemed more promising. And that use of laser weapons remains the most sought-after today. A laser device capable of shooting down a missile also will need to be quite large, but this may not be an obstacle considering that it will not have to be handheld. More problematic is the nature of the lasing medium, the chemical components that produce the laser beam. The lasing mediums used back in the 1960s did not produce beams powerful enough to shoot down enemy aircraft. Later, researchers tried other lasing mediums such as a mixture of the elements fluorine and hydrogen. This produced a lot of power but had some serious problems. The mixture explodes easily and without warning, and the exhaust gas is hard to get rid of and kills anyone who breathes it. Scientists encountered many other such problems over the years.

Scoring Hits at the Speed of Light

But military leaders continued to pour money into laser weapons research. They knew that such weapons would have some clear advantages over normal bullets and missiles. In the first place, when firing a bullet at a moving target one has to aim a bit ahead of the target. This is because the target itself moves ahead while the bullet is racing toward it. Since gravity pulls the bullet downward one also has to aim a bit above the target. In the middle of a battle, with all the smoke, noise, and confusion, hitting a moving target can be a difficult task.

But a laser beam moves at the speed of light. This means that the beam can travel a mile in only six-millionths of a second. Even if an airplane were traveling at the speed of sound, it would move only about one-sixteenth of an inch during the time span in which the laser beam covered the mile. Military experts realized that more hits could be scored by laser weapons than by ordinary guns and missiles. Another potential benefit of beam weapons is that they could be bounced off mirrors, so only the mirrors would need to be moved when switching to a new target (instead of moving the whole weapon). Also, a laser beam stays concentrated over long distances, so it might be able to hit targets hundreds of miles away.

In 1973 the U.S. Army finally succeeded in shooting down a drone (a remote-controlled plane). But military leaders did not consider the test a complete success. The drone did not move as fast as enemy aircraft, and the program leading up to the test had been very expensive. In fact, laser weapons in general seemed to be almost too expensive. At that time a modern tank cost about $1 million to make; experts estimated that a battlefield laser would cost nearly $10 million. But the military still pressed on with laser experiments. By 1980 the U.S. government had spent hundreds of millions of dollars on laser research. Unfortunately, there had been only a few practical results. Looking back, many experts feel the military moved too quickly on lasers. It did not allow enough time for developing the new technology before it demanded results.

Range Finders and Bomb Designators

Still, the military has enjoyed a considerable amount of success in developing laser devices for use on the battlefield. These devices, which greatly improve the accuracy of normal conventional weapons, include range finders and bomb designators. A range finder calculates the distance, or range, to a desired target by measuring how long a small burst of laser light takes to travel to the target. This practical tool can be either handheld or mounted on a tank. Obviously, if a soldier knows the exact distance to his target, he has a much

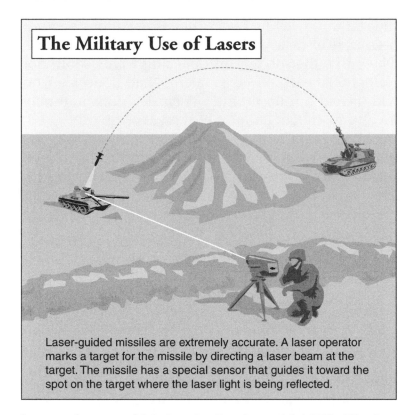

The Military Use of Lasers

Laser-guided missiles are extremely accurate. A laser operator marks a target for the missile by directing a laser beam at the target. The missile has a special sensor that guides it toward the spot on the target where the laser light is being reflected.

better chance of hitting it. By the mid-1970s Hughes Aircraft was building more than $50 million worth of laser range finders for the U.S. military each year.

A laser bomb designator works by shining a low-powered laser beam at the desired target. After the target has been designated, a bomb is released, either from an airplane or from a ground-based missile; this is known as a "smart" bomb because it carries a sensor that can detect the laser beam and use it to home in on and destroy the target. The military first used such devices on the battlefield in 1972 during the Vietnam War, and much improved versions proved highly successful in the Persian Gulf War (in 1991) and especially in the police action against terrorists in Afghanistan (in 2001).

Simulating Battlefield Conditions

Lasers have also proved to be successful in simulating mock battles that are staged to give soldiers practice for the real thing. Before lasers, these simulations had not been as realistic as military officials would have liked. Obviously, the soldiers on opposing teams could not really fire at each other, so referees had to decide who had or had not been "hit." Their decisions naturally involved a certain amount of human error.

In laser battle simulations, soldiers fire special guns that shoot bursts of light. Sensors are attached to each soldier who fights in the battle; such sensors are also attached to tanks, trucks, or any other vehicles used in the mock fighting. When a burst of light is fired and hits a sensor on an "enemy" soldier, the sensor registers the light and everyone knows immediately that the soldier is "dead." They know when a tank or truck has been destroyed because the sensors mounted on vehicles give off a cloud of smoke when hit. Many companies now build such battle simulators, which are used by armies all over the world.

Underwater Communications

Another dramatic use for the military laser is in the area of submarine (underwater) communications. Submarines often patrol in enemy waters, and in the past the only way an admiral could get a message to a sub was by using ordinary radio. But this has two serious disadvantages: First, radio waves do not travel well underwater and require large antennas to broadcast them long distances. Second, there is always the risk that the enemy will pick up the signal, which immediately reveals the sub's location and exposes it to danger.

For underwater use, a laser is more effective than radio because of a unique and important quality of laser light: It is monochromatic. This means that it shines in only one color (*mono* means "one" and *chroma* means "color"). It is very different from ordinary white light, which is made up of all the colors of the rainbow bunched together.

To send a message to a submarine the navy uses a laser that gives off a monochromatic beam of blue-green light. This particular shade of blue-green travels easily through ocean water. The beam carrying the message is transmitted to a satellite orbiting high above the ocean. The satellite then relays the beam down to the sub, which is equipped with a special receiver that registers only blue-green light. In less than a second the sub's computer decodes the signal so the crew can read the message.

If there are any enemy lookouts nearby it is unlikely they will know about the signal beam, which the satellite flashes for only a few millionths of a second. This is not enough time for the lookouts to see the beam with their naked eyes. And even if they have a receiver that detects laser light, it has to be tuned to receive the exact shade of blue-green in the beam. Their receiver

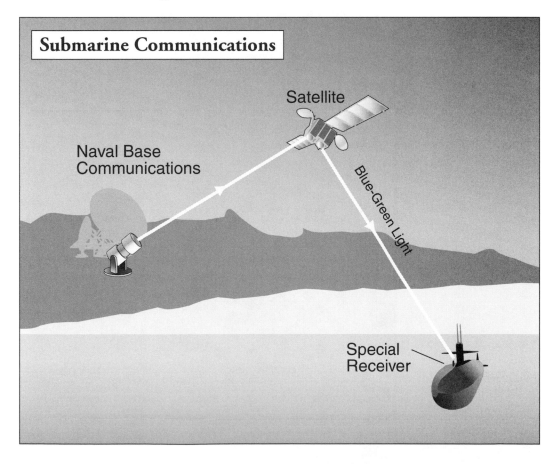

Submarine Communications

Satellite

Naval Base
Communications

Blue-Green Light

Special
Receiver

also has to be underwater near the sub because that is where the satellite aims the beam. Meeting these conditions would be very difficult for the lookouts, so chances are good that the sub will get the message and still remain undetected.

Research on "Star Wars" Continues

Meanwhile, the U.S. military did not give up on developing laser beam weapons. In fact, research into satellite and rocket lasers increased dramatically in the 1980s with President Ronald Reagan's call for the building of a

American researchers stand beside a high-energy laser designed for mounting on a satellite, part of the "Star Wars" weapons program.

defense system nicknamed "Star Wars" after the popular science fiction film series featuring light sabers and other laserlike weapons. The basic idea, which was endorsed by President George W. Bush when he took office in early 2001, is to stop enemy missiles from hitting the United States during a war by destroying them while they are still high above the earth. Laser sensors mounted on satellites would detect incoming missiles and plot their paths. The missiles would then be shot out of the sky, either by beam weapons or by "smart" American missiles that home in on designator beams.

Despite the major difficulties of producing such weapons, a number of military leaders are optimistic that at least a modestly practical version can be built. The U.S. Air Force, for instance, is confident that its ongoing development of the so-called Airborne Laser (ABL) will result in a working weapon within four to six years. "The job of the ABL," reports military weapons observer John Tirpack,

> will be to orbit the skies near the forward edge of a battle area, watching with infrared search-and-track devices for the launch of enemy . . . ballistic missiles. Once it spots one, the ABL platform—a militarized 747 freighter filled with lasers for ranging, targeting, and attack—will get a lock on the target. When the missile rises above the clouds, the ABL will focus a beam of light 15 inches in diameter on the missile's skin. The skin will heat up and rupture, causing the volatile materials inside to explode. Debris—and the missile warhead—will rain down on the nation that launched it. This, it is thought, will serve as a deterrent to the use of . . . ballistic missiles in the first place. As a bonus, the ABL will determine the launch location and then pass that information on to attack airplanes. . . . The strike aircraft can dash to the launch area and destroy other missiles on the ground before the enemy has a chance to fire them or move them to a new hiding place.[5]

At present, the Star Wars defense system remains the subject of debate among scientists, politicians, military personnel, and the American public. Some scientists believe the long-term benefits of such a program are questionable and that the expense involved in implementing it is too high. Others say that Star Wars is necessary to U.S. military strategy against both hostile nations and terrorist attacks and is therefore well worth the money. Whatever the future of Star Wars, the debate is likely to continue for years to come.

There is one thing that everyone can be sure of. Lasers have found a permanent home in the arsenals of the world's armies, so research into the military use of lasers will continue. The wars of the future, as the very successful 2001 U.S. operation in Afghanistan illustrated, will be fought very differently than those of the past. One important difference is that several kinds of laser devices will be standard equipment for large numbers of soldiers, sailors, and pilots.

Chapter 5

Medical Uses of Lasers

In the early days of lasers it came as a surprise that these tools of light could be used in the science of medicine, since no one envisioned that they might be able to heal or otherwise improve people's physical well-being. But doctors and medical researchers quickly began to see the possibilities, and the number of uses for medical lasers multiplied over the years. Among other applications, these include cutting into tissue in surgical procedures; reshaping the cornea of the eye to improve sight; cleaning clogged arteries; burning away cavities and whitening the teeth; removing unwanted hair, wrinkles, birthmarks, and freckles; and reshaping the face in plastic surgery procedures.

The Advent of the "Laser Scalpel"

Early experimenters with medical lasers pointed out that there are surgical operations that are difficult to perform with the conventional scalpel and that a laser beam might be used instead. Initial trials showed that a finely focused beam from a carbon dioxide gas laser could cut through human tissue easily and neatly. The surgeon could direct the beam from any angle by using a mirror mounted on a movable metal arm.

Several advantages of laser surgery quickly became apparent. First, the light beam is consistent, which means that it gives off the same amount of energy from

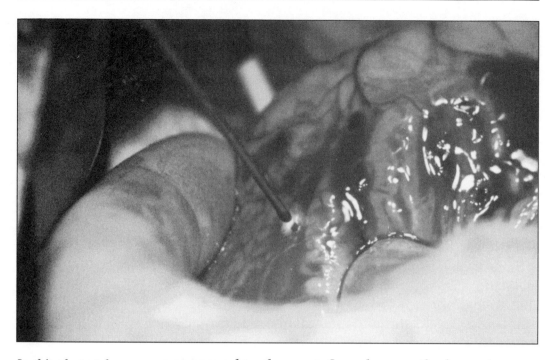

In this photo taken during open-heart surgery, a doctor uses a laser probe to punch small holes in the patient's heart muscle to increase the organ's blood flow.

one second to the next. So as long as the beam is moving along, the cut it makes (the incision) does not vary in depth; whereas when using a scalpel a doctor can accidentally make part of the incision too deep. A second advantage of the surgical laser is that the hot beam cauterizes, or seals off, the open blood vessels as it moves along. (This works well mainly for small vessels, such as those in the skin. The doctor still has to seal off the larger blood vessels using conventional methods.) Still another advantage is that the cells in human tissue do not conduct heat very well, so the skin or any other tissue near the laser incision does not get very hot and is not affected by the beam. This advantage of laser surgery is very helpful when a doctor must operate on a tiny area that is surrounded by healthy tissue or organs.

It should be pointed out that the "laser scalpel" is not necessarily the best tool to use in every operation. Some doctors feel that while the laser is useful in some situations, it will never totally replace the scalpel. Others are more optimistic and see a day when more advanced lasers will make the scalpel a thing of the past.

The second of these views may prove to be the most accurate, for surgical use of lasers is rapidly advancing. At first, lasers were considered most effective in operating on areas that are easy to reach—areas on the body's exterior, including the skin, mouth, nose, ears, and eyes. But in recent years doctors have demonstrated remarkable progress in developing laser techniques for use in internal exploration and surgery. Of course, in order to be able to direct the laser beam the doctor must be able to see inside the body. In some cases this is a simple matter of making an incision and opening up the area to be operated on. But there are situations in which this step can be avoided.

Cleaning Arteries with Light

For instance, lasers are increasingly used to clean plaque from people's arteries. Plaque is a tough fatty substance that can build up on the inside walls of the arteries. Eventually the vessels can get so clogged that blood does not flow normally, and the result can be a heart attack or stroke, both of which are serious and sometimes fatal. The traditional method for removing the plaque involves opening the chest and making several incisions, a long and sometimes risky operation. It is also expensive and requires weeks for recovery.

An effective alternative is to use a laser beam to burn away the plaque. The key to making this work is the doctor's ability to see inside the artery and direct the beam, another area in which fiber optics and lasers are combined into a modern wonder tool. An optic fiber that has been connected to a tiny television camera can be inserted into an artery. These elements now become a miniature sensor that allows the doctor and nurses to see inside the artery while a second fiber is inserted to carry the bursts of light that will burn away the plaque.

The technique works in the following way. The fiber-optic array is inserted into a blood vessel in an arm or leg and moved slowly into the area of the heart and blocked arteries. When the array is in place the laser is fired and the plaque destroyed, and then the exhaust vapors are sucked back through a tiny hollow tube that is inserted along with the optical fibers. When the artery has been cleaned out the doctor removes the fibers and tube, and the operation is finished. This medical process is known as laser angioplasty. It has several obvious advantages. First, no incision is needed (except for the small one in the vessel to insert the fibers). There is also little or no bleeding, and the patient can enjoy total recovery in a day or two.

Laser angioplasty does have some potential risks that must be considered. First, when the laser beam fires at the plaque it must be aimed very carefully because a slight miss could cut through the wall of the artery and cause serious bleeding. The patient's chest would then have to be opened up after all. Another problem involves small pieces of burnt debris from the

Surgeons use a tiny laser to cut away tissue in a gallbladder operation. The laser and a tiny camera are inserted into the navel, so no abdominal incision is necessary.

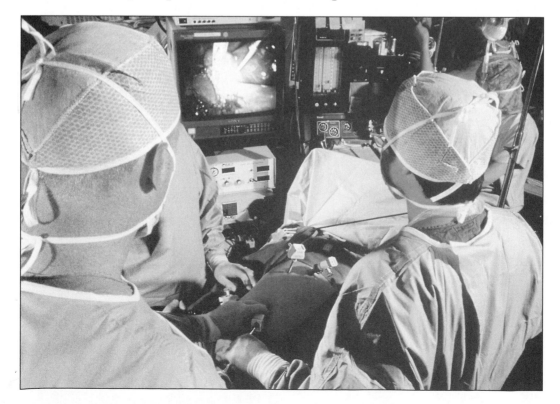

destroyed plaque. If these enter the bloodstream, they can cause blockage in smaller blood vessels, bringing further complications. Fortunately, continuous technical advancements have considerably reduced these risks, and the number of successful laser angioplasties performed is increasing each year.

Lasers Heal and Reshape the Eyes

Some of the most remarkable breakthroughs for medical lasers have been in the area of ophthalmology, the study of the structure and diseases of the eye. One reason that laser beams are so useful in treating the eye is that the cornea, the coating that covers the eyeball and admits light into the interior of the eye, is transparent. Since it is designed to admit ordinary light, the cornea lets in laser light just as well and remains unaffected by the beam.

First, the laser is very useful in removing extraneous blood vessels that can form on the retina—the thin, light-sensitive membrane at the back of the eyeball. It is on the retina that the images of the things the eye sees are formed. Damage to the retina can sometimes cause blindness, the most common form in the United States resulting from diabetes (a disease characterized by high levels of blood sugar) when, in some advanced cases, hundreds of tiny extra blood vessels form on the retina. These block light from the surface of the membrane, resulting in partial or total blindness.

The laser most often used in the treatment of this condition is powered by a medium of argon gas. The doctor aims the beam through the cornea and burns away the tangle of blood vessels covering the retina. The procedure takes only a few minutes and can be done in the doctor's office. The laser can also repair a detached retina—one that has broken loose from the rear part of the eyeball. Before the advent of lasers detached retinas had to be repaired by hand, and because the retina is so delicate this was a very difficult operation to perform. Using the argon laser, the doctor can

Using Lasers for Eye Surgery

The laser works like a sewing machine to repair a detached retina, the membrane that lines the interior of the eye. The laser beam is adjusted so that it can pass harmlessly through the lens and focus on tiny spots around the damaged area of the retina. When it is focused, the beam has the intensity to "weld" or seal the detached area of the retina back against the wall of the eyeball.

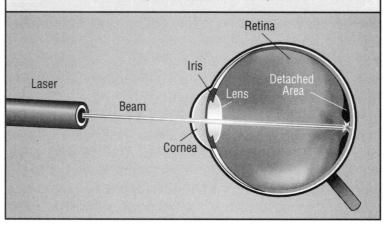

actually "weld" the torn retina back in place. It is perhaps a strange coincidence that Gordon Gould, one of the original inventors of the laser, later had one of his own retinas repaired this way.

Another condition that affects the eye is glaucoma, which is characterized by the buildup of fluid in the eye. Normally the eye's natural fluids drain away a little at a time, and the eye stays healthy. In eyes impaired with glaucoma the fluid does not drain properly, and the buildup affects vision; blindness can sometimes result. In some cases drugs can be used to treat glaucoma. If the drugs fail, however, many doctors now turn to the laser to avoid conventional surgery. The laser punches a hole in a preplanned spot and the fluid drains out through the hole. Again, the treatment can be performed in a doctor's office instead of a hospital.

Perhaps most exciting of all the eye-related laser applications is the reshaping of the eye's cornea, a technique widely known as LASIK (which stands for *Laser-Assisted In Situ Keratomilensis*). As Breck Hitz describes it,

> The patient's eyeglass prescription is literally carved inside the cornea with the beam of an excimer laser [a laser device that produces pulses of ultraviolet, or UV, light]. A small flap of the cornea is first removed with a precision knife . . . and an

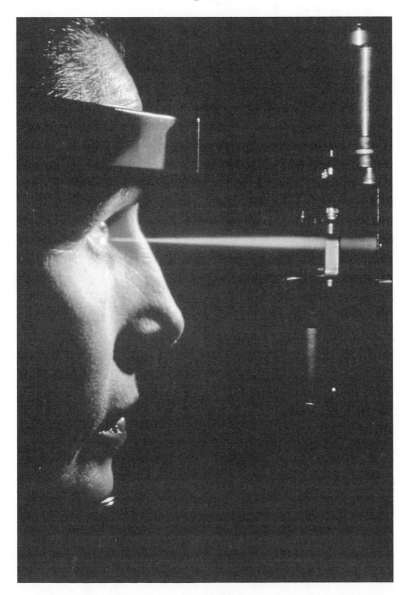

A patient undergoes eye surgery performed by a laser beam. In addition to treating detached retinas, lasers can remove cataracts.

inner portion of the cornea is exposed to the excimer laser. After the prescription is carved, the corneal flap that was opened is then put back into place over the ablated [surgically altered] cornea.[6]

LASIK does not come without risks. The changes it makes in the cornea are permanent, and the danger of unexpected damage is ever present. However, the procedure has become increasingly popular each year; about a million Americans had it done in the year 2000, and about four thousand surgeons in the United States were trained to perform it.

Some Cosmetic Uses of Lasers

Medical lasers are also widely used for various types of cosmetic surgery, including the removal of certain kinds of birthmarks. Port-wine stains, reddish purple skin blotches that appear on about three out of every one thousand children, are an example. Such stains can mark any part of the body but are most commonly found on the face and neck.

The medical laser is able to remove a port-wine stain for the same reason that a military laser is able to flash a message to a submerged submarine. Both lasers take advantage of the monochromatic quality of laser light, that is, its ability to shine in one specific color. The stain is made up of thousands of tiny malformed blood vessels that have a definite reddish purple color. This color very strongly absorbs a certain shade of green light. In fact, that is why the stain looks red. It absorbs the green and other colors in white light but reflects the red back to people's eyes.

To treat the stain, the doctor runs a wide low-power beam of green light across the discolored area. The mass of blood vessels in the stain absorbs the energetic laser light and becomes so hot that it is actually burned away. The surrounding skin is a different color than the stain, so that skin absorbs only small amounts of the beam and remains unburned. (Of course, the burned

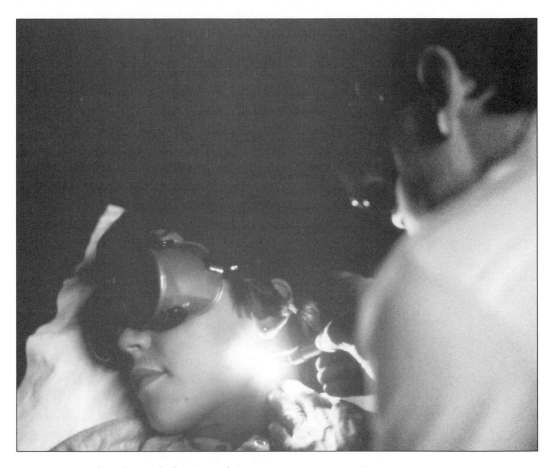

areas must heal, and during this process some minor scarring sometimes occurs.)

A similar method is often successful in removing tattoos. A tattoo is formed when very strong dyes are injected with needles into a person's skin. Someone who has been tattooed may decide later in life that he or she does not want the tattoo anymore; and in the past, the only way to remove these designs involved surgery or burning off the tattoo with acid. Luckily, the laser offers an alternative to such extreme measures. The beam bleaches the dyes in the tattoo without burning the surrounding skin. (As in the case of port-wine stains, some light scarring is possible.)

Still another example of a laser-assisted cosmetic procedure is the removal of unwanted hair. "The laser

A doctor uses an argon laser to remove a port-wine stain, a kind of birthmark. Unwanted tissue is burned away while normal skin remains undamaged.

emits a gentle beam of light," explains Chicago cosmetic surgeon Jeffrey Melton,

> which only is absorbed in the hair follicle (leaving the skin unharmed). The laser delivers energy which is absorbed in the hair and transformed to heat. The heat destroys the hair follicle within a small fraction of a second. . . . Laser hair removal is good for both facial hair removal and for body hair removal. . . . Perhaps the most commonly treated areas are facial hair in women.[7]

Laser-Assisted Dentistry

Dentistry is another branch of medicine that has benefited tremendously from laser technology. Indeed, lasers have made some people stop dreading a visit to the dentist. No one enjoys having a cavity drilled, of course. It usually requires an anesthetic (a painkiller like novocaine) that causes uncomfortable numbness in the mouth; also, the sound of the drill can be irritating or even sickening to some people.

Many dentists now employ an Nd-YAG laser (which uses a crystal for its lasing medium) instead of a drill for most cavities. The laser treatment takes advantage of the simple fact that the material that forms in a cavity is much softer than the enamel (the hard part of a tooth). The laser is set at a power that is just strong enough to eliminate the decayed tissue but not strong enough to harm the enamel. When treating a very deep cavity bleeding sometimes occurs, and the laser beam often seals off blood vessels and stops the bleeding.

The most often asked question about treating cavities with lasers is: Does it hurt? The answer is no. Each burst of laser light from a dental laser lasts only thirty-trillionths of a second, much faster than the amount of time a nerve takes to trigger pain. In other words, the beam would have to last 100 million times longer in order to cause any discomfort. So this sort of treatment requires no anesthetic.

Advantages of Lasers for Dental Surgery

In this excerpt from an article in *The Dental Clinics of North America* Robert A. Strauss of the Medical College of Virginia mentions some of the advantages of using lasers for oral surgery.

Decreased post-operative swelling is characteristic of laser use [for oral surgery]. Decreased swelling allows for increased safety when performing surgery within the airway [the mouth] . . . and increases the range of surgery that oral surgeons can perform safely without fear of airway compromise. This effect allows the surgeon to perform many procedures in an office or outpatient facility that previously would have required hospitalization. . . . Tissue healing and scarring are also improved with the use of the laser. . . . Laser wounds generally heal with minimal scar formation and . . . often can be left unsutured [without stitches], another distinct advantage.

There are literally hundreds of other medical uses for the laser. Still, numerous medical conditions cannot be helped by laser light. And even in those that do respond to laser treatments, a doctor may have a good reason for choosing a different method in a specific case. The plain fact is that, while the laser is a marvelous medical tool, it cannot cure every ill. Yet the world has seen probably only a small fraction of the laser's potential. After all, this supertool has only existed since 1960, and, considering the medical advances it already has created, the future appears promising indeed.

Chapter 6

Lasers in Entertainment

S cientists have found many tasks and uses for lasers. These devices regularly measure, cut, drill, weld, read, write, send messages, solve crimes, carry telephone conversations, burn plaque out of arteries, and perform delicate eye operations. Over and over again the laser has proved to be an extremely practical tool.

Yet lasers have also proved their usefulness in nonpractical applications, especially in the realm of art and entertainment. First and foremost a laser beam is a wand of light; and light itself can be beautiful as well as practical. The sight of a deep red sunset or multicolored rainbow often inspires feelings of happiness, romance, and even awe. For centuries artists have tried to reproduce light's beauty in paintings, and inventors have given artists mechanical tools such as the camera, which uses light to create art that is entertaining (as in the motion picture) as well as beautiful. Because the laser produces a special kind of light, early in the laser era people realized its potential to create special kinds of art and entertainment. And today, lasers are involved in almost all aspects of these fields, from "light shows" to compact discs (CDs) and digital video discs (DVDs), to special effects in the movies.

Spectacular Combinations of Light and Music
Back in the 1960s when lasers were still relatively new, artists began to use them to produce "light paintings."

These took the form of one-time performances in which an artist flashed laser beams in various ways to create visually striking patterns. The beams might be bounced off mirrors placed in preplanned positions or attached to the artist, who would move about, reflecting the rays against walls, glass objects, or into tanks

A huge crowd enjoys a laser show projected onto the granite surface of Stone Mountain near Atlanta, Georgia.

filled with liquid. Another variation involved bouncing the beams against clouds of machine-made fog. Usually the performance was done to music. The effects of these displays could often be exciting to watch, especially at night when the beams glowed brightly against the dark sky.

Unfortunately, not many artists could afford the equipment necessary for light paintings. So it became more common for organizations to stage and charge admission fees to see such displays in public performances, which came to be called light shows. The first recorded public laser show took place at Mills College in Oakland, California, on May 9, 1969. Large fairs and celebrations also began to present displays of laser art. The same group that created the Mills College show put on a much more spectacular version in 1970 at the Pepsi-Cola Pavilion at Expo '70 in Osaka, Japan. More than 2 million people attended.

At the Expo '70 show the laser artists set up rotating mirrors and wired them to equipment that played music. They aimed four colored laser beams—red, yellow, green, and blue—at the mirrors. When the music played, the sounds traveled through the wires and caused the mirrors to spin at different speeds; and the mirrors bounced the beams around the room in complex patterns, sometimes to the beat of the music. Many of the spectators reported that the combination of light and music was breathtakingly beautiful.

A much more spectacular display of laser art occurred during the U.S. bicentennial celebration staged at the Washington Monument in 1976. An audience of 4 million people watched the show up close, and the beams could be seen twenty miles away. Other laser artists staged two such large-scale presentations in 1980, one to help celebrate the city of Boston's 350th birthday, the other to enliven a huge party in honor of President Ronald Reagan's inauguration.

In these major laser shows the light beams could be considered the main attraction; the music supported the visual display. But it soon became clear to people in the music business that the reverse could work just as well. Thus it became common to witness laser shows at music concerts, especially rock concerts. In such cases the music performance is the main attraction, while the laser light show takes on the supporting role. Many well-known rock groups and other recording artists have staged these light shows at their concerts; The Who was the first group to do so and Pink Floyd became particularly famous for its laser shows.

From time to time there have been some questions about safety during rock concert laser shows. Some of the early displays allowed the beams to shine into the audience, which was potentially dangerous; the beams are not powerful enough to burn a person's skin, but if a beam shines directly into someone's eye a permanent blind spot can form. Because of this danger a number of countries have established strict rules about how lasers can be used in concerts.

Laser Discs Create a Revolution

While the laser continues to thrill people in large visual shows, it also entertains them on a small scale in their homes. In the late 1970s and early 1980s a revolution in viewing and listening technology began. First came the videodisc player, which plays movies and other shows on a television screen. The disc was encoded with the visual information (the movie) in roughly the same way that computer storage discs are encoded. A laser beam burns patterns into a film that covers the disc and later a small laser inside the player scans the disc and relays the picture to the screen. The picture produced by a videodisc is brighter and sharper than the one produced by a videotape.

Unfortunately, the first videodisc players that came on the market had many problems. A great many had not been built well, and buyers returned them; also, the companies that built them did not make and supply a wide enough variety of movie titles to satisfy customers.

Many more titles existed on videotape, and tape players themselves seemed more reliable; so laser videodiscs did not immediately catch on with consumers.

As experts worked to eliminate the bugs from videodisc technology, laser audio discs, which came to be called compact discs, or CDs, hit the market. These did catch on quickly with the public and rapidly replaced traditional long-playing records. One reason for the success of the CD is its excellent sound reproduction. In a phonograph a needle comes in direct contact with the carved grooves on the surface of the record, and the more the record is played the more the grooves wear down. In addition, they can hold only a certain amount of musical information.

In a CD player, by contrast—either audio or video—only a beam of laser light touches the surface of the disc. Barring accidents or misuse, therefore, the discs do not wear out. Moreover, they carry much more information than records and the sound is sharper and more realistic. The other reasons for the success of audio CDs are the same as for the early success of videotapes over

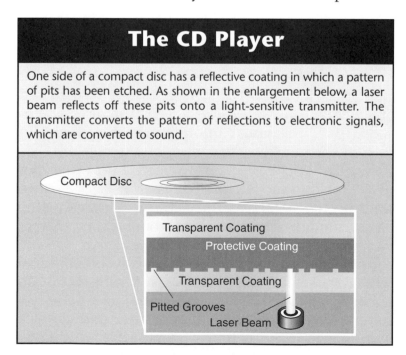

The CD Player

One side of a compact disc has a reflective coating in which a pattern of pits has been etched. As shown in the enlargement below, a laser beam reflects off these pits onto a light-sensitive transmitter. The transmitter converts the pattern of reflections to electronic signals, which are converted to sound.

Compact Disc

Transparent Coating
Protective Coating
Transparent Coating
Pitted Grooves
Laser Beam

videodiscs. The audio CD players proved to be largely reliable, few customers returned them, and manufacturers quickly made tens of thousands of titles available. In fact, many titles appeared on discs that could not be found on traditional records.

The Videodisc Comeback and DVDs

Meanwhile, videodisc technology, which had been down but not out, made a comeback. By the early 1990s researchers had considerably improved the technology and produced far more reliable players with disc-produced pictures sharper and more realistic than ever. Furthermore, in an effort to attract new customers, manufacturers offered a wider range of titles and also introduced the concept of deluxe editions of movies. The deluxe versions, which have become almost standard today, often include restored footage (scenes that appeared in the original film but got lost over the years) as well as behind-the-scenes footage of the making of the film, and even outtakes (bloopers).

Later in the 1990s a newer, even more improved version of the laser videodisc—the *d*igital *v*ideo *d*isc, or DVD—appeared. The DVD produces a sharper, more defined picture than either a standard videotape or a laser CD. This is because a videotape picture breaks down into 210 individual horizontal lines, while a CD picture has 425 lines and a DVD picture 540 lines; the more lines, the sharper the image. Expert Rich D'Ambrise explains other superior qualities of DVD:

> DVD discs make CDs look like the 5^1/$_4$ inch floppy [computer] discs of earlier times. Just a single-sided, single-layer DVD disc offers 4.7 GB [gigabytes, each gigabyte equal to 1,000 megabytes, or MBs] of capacity, which is worlds away from a CD's 680 MB capacity. When we start discussing the 17 GB capacity of a double-sided, dual-layer DVD, it's like comparing the scribbles of a one-year-old toddler to a Monet masterpiece. What makes DVD superior

to its CD counterpart is the manufacturing process and internal design. . . . Two injection molds are required to make one DVD, which consists of two banded 0.6 mm discs [as opposed to one in a CD].[8]

DVD laser technology had become immensely popular in an extremely short time span. By the close of 2001 an estimated 22 million DVD players had been sold; in that same year the film *Shrek* sold a record 2.5 million DVDs, soon surpassed by *How the Grinch Stole Christmas* with sales of 3 million.

The Advent of Holographic Images

Another form of laser light–produced art and entertainment is called holography, a special type of photography that creates three-dimensional pictures. By contrast, a standard camera produces pictures that are only two-dimensional. Holography began to develop in the late 1940s, quite a while before lasers appeared. The basic idea was to shine two separate beams of light at a sensitive sheet of photographic film. One beam would bounce off the object being photographed while the other would travel a different path, and both beams would reach the sheet of film at the same time. Once exposed by the light, the film itself became the hologram. Later, when a person shined a third beam at the hologram, a three-dimensional picture of the object was supposed to be visible.

The idea made sense in theory, but it was very difficult to construct a working model. One problem was that the light in the beams had to be coherent, moving along with all the waves in step. Another problem was that both beams had to be monochromatic. Producing two identical beams with these properties was an almost impossible task at that time. Researchers tried all kinds of light sources, but none worked very well and progress in holography was slow all through the 1950s.

Then, in 1960 Theodore Maiman built his ruby laser and holography received a sudden boost. Researchers

Holography

Holograms are photographs that look three dimensional. Objects in a hologram appear to move when viewed from different angles. A hologram is made by directing a laser beam at the object to be photographed. Between the laser and the object, however, is a half-silvered mirror, or beam splitter, which splits the laser beam in two. One of the beams, called the reference beam, is reflected directly from the mirror to the photographic plate. The other, the object beam, first passes through the mirror. Then it reflects off the object and onto the photographic plate. The interference between these two beams when they meet on the photographic plate causes the three-dimensional effect of the hologram.

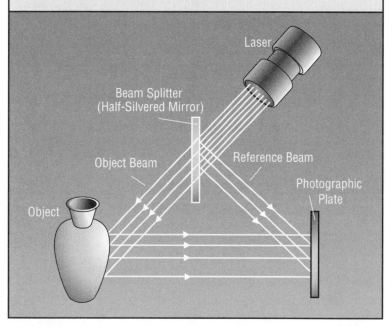

now had a light source that was bright, coherent, and monochromatic. They found that they could produce two identical laser beams by passing a single laser beam through a device called a beam splitter. These beams bounced off a series of mirrors to reach the photographic film.

Almost everyone has seen a hologram at one time or another. The three-dimensional images on credit cards are holograms, as are the many three-dimensional characters and objects portrayed in arcade video games.

Sometimes these images seem so real that the spectator invariably reaches out to touch them, only to be reminded that they are illusions.

Some technical problems with holography remain. Objects that are too big cannot be photographed very well. And because monochromatic light must be used, the images produced are in one color. The only way to make multicolored pictures is by combining several different-colored laser beams, which is very difficult to do. The images made this way do not look completely natural. Also, air molecules absorb some of the light and cause the pictures to look grainy. But scientists are working to overcome these problems.

Artists have tried working with holograms but, as with lasers, the equipment is expensive. So holographic art is not yet widespread. A more practical art-related use for holography is in examining ancient

This hologram, a three-dimensional image created by passing laser light through a beam splitter, shows a space shuttle orbiting Earth.

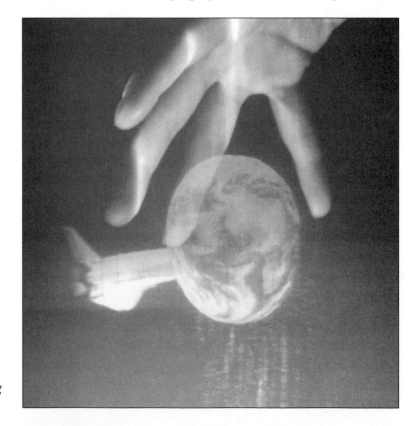

paintings. When an old masterpiece is photographed to produce a hologram, experts can detect which sections of the painting are in need of repair.

Laser Movie Magic

Still another use for lasers in the entertainment field is the production of special effects for movies. Several companies that produce these effects (usually referred to as "special effects houses") use lasers in highly technical ways to help make their equipment produce truer colors. The first movie to use a laser to print images directly onto the film was *Young Sherlock Holmes,* released in 1985. Industrial Light and Magic (ILM), perhaps the most famous special effects house, created the effects for the film. In one scene a painted knight on a stained glass church window comes to life. The knight jumps down from the window and chases a priest out of church.

The effect was created in the following way: ILM artists painted the knight onto a TV screen using a special pen that used electricity instead of ink or paint. The image was then stored in a computer that was hooked up to the screen. Next, the artists programmed the computer to rearrange the image so it could be seen from several different angles. Then the computer created pictures of each of the different movements the knight would make in the finished scene. When the artists ordered the computer to play back all these images quickly, the knight appeared to move around on the computer screen.

In the last and most important step the artists transferred the computer images of the knight onto the photographic film. In creating similar effects for previous movies this was done by simply photographing the images directly from the computer screen. But the picture on a computer screen is not as sharp and bright as filmmakers would like, so the ILM artists decided to connect the computer to a laser. The computer directed the laser to transfer, or "paint," the stored images of the knight right onto the blank film. The knight now showed more detail, and the colors were much more vivid. Later, this film clip of the moving knight was combined with separate film footage of the priest in the church. In the final version that appeared on theater screens the knight seemed to be actually walking around inside the church.

Many later movies have employed this and other laser techniques. The blockbuster *Jurassic Park 3,* for example, used a laser to create computerized models of the dinosaurs that run amok in the film. First, technicians made a small clay model (called a maquette) of a dinosaur; then they ran a laser beam across the maquette's surface, and the beam transferred highly detailed images of it into a computer. Later, animators used highly sophisticated computer animation programs to make the computer images come to life.

These examples illustrate the use of lasers behind the scenes. But what about lasers *on screen*? As strange as it might sound, when moviemakers want to portray an actual laser beam on the screen, they cannot use a real laser. For instance, contrary to popular opinion the laser swords used by Luke Skywalker and other characters in the *Star Wars* films were not lasers at all.

There are a number of reasons why such on-screen laser beams have to be faked. First, real laser devices would not produce beams only three feet long; instead, the beams would keep on going and punch holes in the furniture, walls, and bodies of innocent onlookers. Also, the effect of the two beams smashing together like regular metal swords is completely imaginary. Real laser beams would just pass right through each other, an image that would make a movie fight appear disconcerting and more comical than dramatic. The most obvious problem with using real lasers (if such handheld versions could even be built) would be the danger posed by the brightness of the beams. The actors and most of the members of the film crew would all be blind within an hour. For the moment,

Science Fiction Lasers Perpetuate Misconceptions

Science fiction movies not only utilize lasers in creating their special effects but also regularly depict lasers or laserlike devices. Unfortunately these portrayals of laser light are often inaccurate for the sake of dramatic effect; and this perpetuates several common misconceptions about lasers, as pointed out here by J.P. Talbot in his article "Lasers in the Movies Reality Check: Science vs. Science Fiction."

Let's speculate on what would actually happen if you were a member of a large fleet of friendly ships engaging enemy ships in a laser beam battle in space. . . . Science Fiction: You fire a laser weapon at the enemy and you "see" and "hear" the beam emerging from your laser gunports (which violently recoil) and watch the "beam" travel very fast toward the enemy ship, which promptly bursts into flames and explodes very loudly (a sound that you hear instantaneously). Science Fact: You quietly fire an invisible beam from a laser weapon without recoil. . . . Your laser beam travels at the speed of light [so you could not watch it travel]. . . . Sound doesn't travel through a vacuum [so you would hear neither the laser discharge nor the explosion]. . . . Most space ships don't "burst" into flames since there's no air in space to sustain such explosive combustion.

therefore, the depiction of laser beams on film must be accomplished though more traditional kinds of special effects.

Still, real lasers have added a fresh, visually exciting dimension to the world of entertainment. In the years to come it is certain that scientists and artists will continue to combine their talents to produce many inventive and dramatic new forms of laser-based entertainment.

Chapter 7

The Future of the Laser

Modern technology is advancing so quickly that the average person simply cannot keep up with it. Even some scientists are occasionally unaware of discoveries being made in other fields. Lasers are very much a part of this technology explosion. They help in the discovery of new knowledge, which further fuels the explosion while, by advancing communications, they help spread the new knowledge to those who want it.

No one can predict what new and unheard-of discoveries will mark the next century of science. These discoveries no doubt will change the world in ways that cannot even be guessed at. What can be imagined are possible ways that today's technology might be used in the near future. In the case of the laser, consider what projects are in the development stages now and what other projects experts see on the immediate horizon.

Realistic Images in Homes and Offices

Many experts expect laser-computer advances to lead to the eventual perfection of holography, for example. By some estimates, within twenty years three-dimensional holographic movies will become common. It will be like watching old-fashioned 3D movies, only without the special glasses. Even holographic television will likely be developed, although it will be very difficult to construct because so much information is needed to form a holographic image. To transmit the information of a single hologram to a home, it will take a cable with the capacity of five hundred television channels. Once the hologram arrives in someone's living room, the television itself will have to be able to project the hologram, and this will require a screen with more than one thousand times more detail than today's TV screens.

But many researchers believe these problems will be solved. If so, it will mean that more than entertainment can be piped into a person's home. When the phone rings, for instance, a projected image of the caller could appear in the room, an illusion that would seem perfectly real (except, of course, that the person receiving the call would be able to walk right through the image of the caller). Once perfected, this amazing technology will not be limited to telephone calls. Business meetings will be held in which only a few or even none of the participants are actually in the meeting room. Similarly, a teacher's hologram might be

Computing at Light Speed

In the mid-1990s the laser joined in a useful working partnership with the computer, but the laser still only reads, writes, and memorizes for the computer. Some scientists think the laser could go further and bring about a drastic change in the way the computer is designed. The computer itself consists of wires, chips, connections, and other parts through which electrical signals flow. Experts point out that in the larger supercomputers sometimes too many pieces of information try to get to the same place at the same time. Due to the limitations of the machine parts themselves, the information bits can only move so fast. As a result, bottlenecks form. These are like miniature traffic jams, only with bits of data instead of cars. The laser might be able to eliminate such bottlenecks by using light instead of electricity to process the information. A laser beam could carry millions of signals without once touching a physical connection. Thus bottlenecks would be eliminated and much more information could flow through the computer. Many technical problems need to be worked out before such an optical computer can be built. But researchers around the world are presently trying to solve these problems.

made to appear in the bedroom of a student who is home sick.

Of course, such a system could be seriously misused. For example, a disreputable government or organization could secretly plant a holograph camera in a person's home and then spy on the person by watching a completely three-dimensional hologram of his or her every movement. At the very least, this could be an embarrassing situation. It is hoped that if such technology becomes common, safeguards will be developed to discourage such invasions of privacy.

Walking Electronics Stores?

Advanced laser-based devices may also transform ordinary people into virtual walking electronics stores. The fact that the beam of a laser can be focused to a microscopic point has already given it the ability to create discs to store vast amounts of information, including video and audio discs of high quality. Researchers are now working to expand this principle to the miniaturization of electronic devices so that they can be carried or even worn by the average person. A tiny disc programmed with billions of bits of information will become the core of each device. The devices themselves will have to be modified to work with fiber optics or some other system that eliminates conventional metal wires and circuits. This will allow the machines to be extremely small.

The end result will be a tiny unit, probably worn like a standard watch or carried in a pocket or purse. Such a unit will include a telephone, television, radio, tape recorder and player, and a wireless hookup to the Internet. Instead of using a bulky monitor screen, a tiny laser within the unit will project images from the television, tape player, or Internet onto any blank surface the wearer desires or perhaps in the air in the form of a laser hologram. Such a gadget will be the direct precursor of the "tricorder," the futuristic device that allows the characters of *Star Trek* to gather, access, and analyze all manner of information.

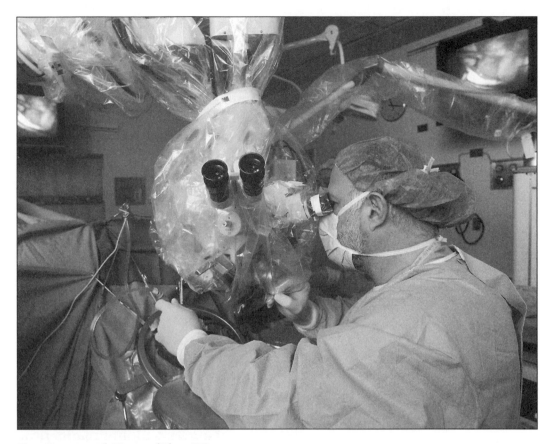

Brains and Eyes like New

Another *Star Trek* device uses beams of light to heal wounds, broken bones, and internal injuries. In a similar vein, doctors have already begun to use lasers in brain surgery for procedures such as burning away a tumor that has formed within the skull. Some researchers are hopeful that many other types of delicate brain operations will be performed with lasers. Some such treatments may use low-power laser light to cause chemical reactions in selected sections of brain tissue, reactions that might help control certain mental disorders.

The future of lasers in eye surgery already promises to bring about a world in which no one needs eyeglasses or contact lenses. Reshaping the cornea with laser light is now a common medical procedure; but in

A doctor removes a brain tumor by aiming a laser beam at the tumor. The exposed brain is visible on surrounding monitor screens.

only a few years doctors will be able to go further and completely reshape the human eye using laser beams. One beam will precisely measure the eye in three dimensions to pinpoint any problems and feed the information into a computer, which will figure out exactly how the eye should be reshaped. The doctor then will use a different beam to cut the eyeball at various strategic points and another beam to weld the incisions together. Eventually, the eyeball will be shaped correctly, and the person will be able to see with perfect twenty-twenty vision.

The Dream of Unlimited Energy

An even more ambitious and far-reaching future use for the laser will be the production of energy, mainly in the form of electricity to power homes, factories, offices, and machines. Today's major sources of energy are water power; the burning of coal, gas, and oil; and nuclear reactors. But all these methods may not be enough to supply the energy needs of the future. The population of the world continues to grow rapidly, and more people create a demand for more energy. Moreover, water power requires building plants near rivers or dams; there are only so many such locations and most are not very near population centers. Meanwhile, supplies of coal, gas, and oil are running out, and nuclear reactors can leak radiation, creating a public danger. Disposing of spent nuclear materials is also a big problem. It is no wonder, then, that no new nuclear plants are presently planned in the United States.

The laser, on the other hand, promises to open up new and seemingly endless stores of energy for humanity's use. Production of energy by lasers will take two forms, the first being the solar-powered satellite. The satellite will be rocketed into a special orbital position where it will always stay above a certain fixed point on Earth's surface. Once in position the satellite will begin gathering energy from sunlight. The energy will power a large laser that will direct a beam back to Earth where a receiver will collect the beam and convert it into electricity. If enough of these satellites can be put into orbit, a large share of Earth's energy needs will be met.

Some people worry that such a beam might be aimed in the wrong direction and cause death and destruction. As a matter of fact, the military has considered this method for making beam weapons. But ways will be found to adjust the power of the beam so that it will not do any damage. The time and money it will take to get these satellites orbiting will be worthwhile because sunlight is free. And because the sun is expected to shine for several billion more years, sunlight is also nearly inexhaustible.

The Power of the Atom

The other way lasers will produce energy is by facilitating nuclear fusion, the process that makes the sun and other stars shine. Fusion is one of two processes that are normally referred to as atomic, the other being nuclear fission. Both of these processes have been successfully used by scientists to make atomic bombs. (Fission produced the atom bomb, and fusion produced the hydrogen bomb.)

Nuclear fission occurs when a subatomic particle (such as a neutron) hits the center, or nucleus, of an atom. The nucleus splits, sending out other particles plus a burst of energy. These particles then hit other atoms, the process quickly speeds up, and as more and more atoms are split a chain reaction takes place, releasing vast amounts of energy in the form of heat and light. This large release of energy destroyed the cities of Hiroshima and Nagasaki in Japan in 1945. These bombings, which killed hundreds of thousands of people, brought an end to World War II. Later, scientists learned how to produce fission on a smaller scale. Since they now could control the process, they called it a controlled reaction. Controlled reactions

Lasers and Nuclear Fusion

Most nuclear scientists believe that in the future nuclear power will be supplied by fusion, a nuclear reaction in which two atoms are combined. But starting a fusion reaction requires an enormous initial force. Many scientists think that "laser chains" can supply that force. A laser chain consists of several laser amplifiers over a hundred feet long, which intensify the power of laser beams. The high-powered beams are directed through beam splitters and onto mirrors so that several beams strike a tiny fuel pellet from all sides at once. This causes an explosion powerful enough to trigger a fusion reaction.

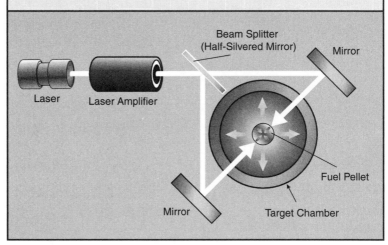

are created at nuclear power plants where the energy produced is converted into electricity. But such reactions give off large amounts of dangerous radiation, which has prompted scientists to search for other safer sources of energy.

The other nuclear process, fusion, occurs when two separate atoms are violently forced together. The structure of the atoms breaks down and a new, heavier atom is formed. In the process, large amounts of energy are released as a by-product. In the sun and other stars, hydrogen atoms fuse to become helium atoms, and energy in the form of heat and light is released. One great benefit of controlling fusion for energy production is that the process is relatively clean and safe. All that is needed for fuel is a small amount of hydrogen, which can be found in ordinary seawater; so the fuel is cheap and the supply almost endless. In addition, the process does not leak dangerous radiation, as fission does.

Scientists have not yet been able to produce controlled fusion reactions of any consequence. This is because fusion requires a large amount of energy just to get the process going. (In the sun, the trigger is the tremendous heat in the interior of the star itself. The trigger used to ignite a hydrogen bomb is an atom bomb.)

The laser may provide a way to get a safe fusion reaction going. Experiments with lasers and fusion began in the late 1960s, but progress was slow for a long time. A major breakthrough occurred in August 2001 when researchers from Japan and the United Kingdom succeeded in using a laser beam to compress a ball-like

Twenty-four lasers are arranged for a nuclear fusion experiment. Controlled fusion has not yet been perfected, but lasers may open the door to that important new technology.

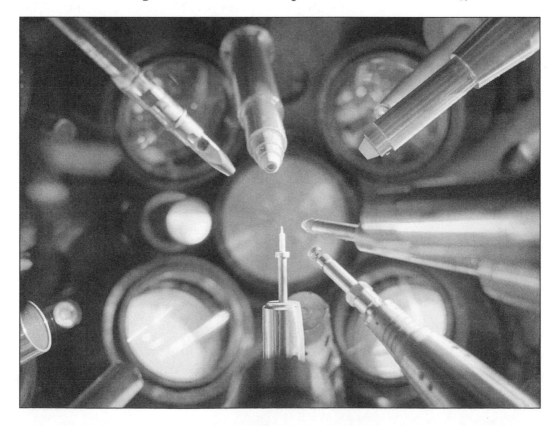

pellet of nuclear fuel. The beam, which generated temperatures of 10 million degrees centigrade, focused on the pellet, creating enormous pressure—about 10 million times that of Earth's atmosphere. The pressure caused the pellet to implode (collapse inward) and release energy.

The energy generated in this experiment is not enough to power machines and houses, so the advent of large-scale controlled fusion still lies in the future. But increasingly advanced lasers may bring that future much closer than ever before dreamed—perhaps in only a few decades rather than centuries, as once predicted.

Searching for ET

An even more futuristic and quite intriguing use for advanced lasers is to aid in the detection of extraterrestrial civilizations on planets orbiting distant stars. The idea of flashing lasers to alert our presence to extraterrestrials is not new. But only recently was a laser built with the high power needed to do the job. According to science reporter Seth Shostak:

> Scientists at Lawrence Livermore National Laboratory, in California, have built a laser capable of putting out light pulses with a power of 1,000 trillion watts, although the pulses are brief: only a trillionth of a second long. It is called Nova and it's not your daddy's laser pointer. Imagine . . . taking aim at a star system 50 light-years away. . . . Every pulse . . . will eventually deliver about 10 photons [of light] per square meter onto the planets of the neighboring star system. . . . During the laser transmitter's short duty cycle, it outshines the Sun by a factor of thirty thousand.[9]

The interstellar laser communicator works both ways, of course. Earth scientists may be able to detect high-energy laser pulses sent out by their alien counterparts. Specially designed light receptors on Earth

potentially could detect the telltale photons of an alien laser, proving that an extraterrestrial civilization exists and wants to set up a dialogue.

A World Transformed

In 1905 when Albert Einstein described the then unknown process of stimulated photon emission, he and other scientists did not foresee the invention of the laser and its fantastic number of uses. As has happened so many times in the history of science, one person's idea grew to transform the world. And this transformation will surely continue.

In the twenty-first century and beyond, the laser promises to help raise human civilization to new heights. The supertool will build a storehouse of knowledge and put that knowledge within easy reach of most people. Laser light will illuminate a complex

Technicians inspect the inside of the Nova laser, built by the Lawrence Livermore National Laboratory. When activated, the beam is thousands of times brighter than the sun.

and computerized world, one in which technology allows men and women to live increasingly productive and happy lives. Indeed, the laser may one day harness the fire of the stars to give humanity clean, safe, and abundant energy for generations to come as well as access to alien knowledge that could transform the world in ways not yet imagined.

Notes

Chapter 2: Lasers in Science and Industry

1. Breck Hitz et al., *Introduction to Laser Technology*. New York: Institute of Electrical and Electronics Engineers, 2001, p. 3.
2. Michael Berns, "Laser Scissors and Tweezers," *Scientific American*, April 1998. www.sciam.com, p. 5.

Chapter 3: Lasers in Communication and Marketing

3. National Academy of Engineers, "Laser and Fiber Optics," December 2000. www.greatachievements.org, p. 18.

Chapter 4: Military Applications of Lasers

4. Hitz et al., *Introduction to Laser Technology*, p. 5.
5. John A. Tirpack, "Military Lasers High and Low," *Air Force Magazine*, September 1999. www.afa.org, pp. 1–2.

Chapter 5: Medical Uses of Lasers

6. Hitz et al., *Introduction to Laser Technology*, p. 252.
7. Jeffrey Melton, "Laser Hair Removal," University of Chicago, Department of Dermatology, accessed November 27, 2001. www.drmelton.com, p. 6.

Chapter 6: Lasers in Entertainment

8. Rich D'Ambrise, "A Closer Look at DVD," Maxell Corporation of America, accessed December 6, 2001. www.cd-info.com, p. 1.

Chapter 7: The Future of the Laser

9. Seth Shostak, "In Search of Aliens," *Space.com*, June 14, 2001. www.space.com, pp. 1–2.

For Further Reading

Books

Mary V. Fox, *Lasers*. Tarrytown, NY: Benchmark Books, 1996. Aimed at young readers, this is a good general introduction to the subject.

Nina Morgan, *Lasers*. New York: Raintree/Steck Vaughn, 1997. The author explains in general terms how lasers work and discusses a number of the modern applications of the technology.

Internet Sources

Erik Baard, "Tool Time in Space: Drilling with Lasers and Ultrasound," *Space.com,* September 19, 2001. www.space.com. Tells how scientists plan to study and mine asteroids and comets by drilling into them with lasers.

Ron Kurtus, "Lasers," *School for Champions,* October 6, 1999. www.school-for-champions.com. A brief but informative tutorial about how lasers work.

Katie Pennicott, "Lasers Illuminate the Flight of the Bumblebee," *Physics Web,* October 16, 2001. http://physicsweb.org. How lasers cleverly measured the strokes of a bee's wings, showing scientists the unique way these insects fly.

Seth Shostak, "In Search of Aliens," *Space.com,* June 14, 2001. www.space.com. Discusses the real possibility of communicating with alien civilizations by using laser beams, which can carry huge amounts of information.

John Watson, "Lasers," University of Aberdeen, Engineering Department, January 8, 1997. http://vcs.abdn.ac.uk. A thorough but understandable explanation of how lasers work.

Matthew Weschler, "How Lasers Work," *Marshall Brain's How Stuff Works,* accessed November 27, 2001. www.howstuffworks.com. Explains the basics of the atom, how atoms relate to lasers, and the different types of lasers.

Works Consulted

Books

Robert A. Convissar, ed., *The Dental Clinics of North America: Lasers and Light Amplification in Dentistry.* Philadelphia: W.B. Saunders, 2000. A collection of detailed, scholarly essays on various aspects of laser-based dental procedures.

Jeff Hecht, *City of Light: The Story of Fiber Optics.* New York: Oxford University Press, 1999. An excellent summary of fiber-optics technology.

Breck Hitz et al., *Introduction to Laser Technology.* New York: Institute of Electrical and Electronics Engineers, 2001. An advanced technical overview of lasers, including how they work and the configuration and uses of different types of lasers.

Clifford L. Lawrence, *The Laser Book—A New Technology of Light.* New York: Prentice-Hall, 1986. Though dated in some of its details, this remains a useful general introduction to lasers.

John F. Ready, *Industrial Applications of Lasers.* San Diego: Academic Press, 1997. A detailed, scholarly discussion of laser use in welding, drilling, cutting, surface treatment, holography, fiber optics, and more.

Thomas G. Smith, *Industrial Light and Magic: The Art of Special Effects.* New York: Ballantine Books, 1991. An excellent synopsis of special effects for movies created by the leading special effects house in Hollywood.

Myron L. Wolbarsht, *Laser Applications in Medicine and Biology.* London: Plenum, 2000. A detailed, scholarly discussion of the use of laser technology for surgery and biological research.

Periodicals

C. Booth, "Cosmetic Surgery: Light Makes Right," *Time,* October 11, 1999. Discusses using laser beams to eliminate wrinkles and perform other kinds of cosmetic surgery.

R.J. Newman, "The New Space Race," *U.S. News & World Report,* November 8, 1999. How advanced high-power lasers will fit into the "Star Wars" missile defenses proposed by some U.S. leaders.

R. Saltus, "Zap! Clearer Vision, Healthier Teeth," *Good Housekeeping,* October 1998. A brief overview of the use of lasers in eye surgery and dentistry.

R.F. Service, "Lighting the Way to a Quantum Computer," *Science,* June 29, 2001. The possibility of computers that will run via photons or pulses of laser light is discussed here.

B.A. Smith, "Thel Laser Kills Short-Range Missile," *Aviation Week and Space Technology,* June 12, 2000. New advances in military lasers.

C. Trumble, "Fiber Optics sans the Fiber," *Smart Computing,* August 2000. Possible creation of fiber-optic technology using airborne, rather than cable-borne, lasers.

Internet Sources

American Society of Plastic Surgeons, "Lasers in Plastic Surgery," *Plastic Surgery Information Service,* accessed November 27, 2001. www.plasticsurgery.org. An overview of the basic techniques of plastic surgery using laser beams, including "resurfacing" to eliminate wrinkles.

Tim Beardsley, "Making Light Work," *Scientific American,* August 1997. www.sciam.com. Explains how lasers can be used to make precision metal parts.

Michael Berns, "Laser Scissors and Tweezers," *Scientific American,* April 1998. www.sciam.com. Tells how scientists use lasers both to hold microscopic objects and to manipulate them.

Ching-Wu Chu, "Laser," *Microsoft Encarta,* 2001. http://encarta. msn.com. A general synopsis of laser operation and applications.

Rich D'Ambrise, "A Closer Look at DVD," Maxell Corporation of America, accessed December 6, 2001. www.cd-info.com. A straightforward explanation of the difference between CD and DVD technology, both of which employ lasers.

Andrew Gannon, "Lasers Split the Atom," *Focus,* January 21, 2000. http://focus.aps.org. Explains recent breakthroughs that will allow scientists to use lasers in conducting new kinds of nuclear physics experiments.

Corey Grice, "Lasers Beat Bandwidth Bottleneck," *ZDNet News,* February 22, 2001. www.zdnet.com. Discusses efforts to use lasers to increase the amount of information carried by optical wireless technology.

David Harris, "All About Lasers," *About: The Human Internet,* accessed November 27, 2001. http://physics.about.com. A very lucid explanation of the workings of lasers, supplemented by several colorful, informative diagrams by the author.

Murray McFadden, "Laser Eye Surgery," *LASIK & PRK Today,* October 23, 2000. www.prk.com. Lists a wide range of sources providing information on the latest developments in laser eye surgery.

Jeffrey Melton, "Freckle Removal by Laser" and "Laser Hair Removal," University of Chicago, Department of Dermatology, accessed November 27, 2001. www.drmelton.com. Two among several articles posted by the University of Chicago explaining various medical/cosmetic uses of lasers.

National Academy of Engineers, "Laser and Fiber Optics," December 2000. www.greatachievements.org. An easy-to-read general synopsis of the history and present uses of laser fiber optics.

Dieter Schuocker, "Lasers: An Overview," *Nonconventional Processing, Forming, and Laser Technology,* accessed December 3, 2001. www.argelas.org. A general, scholarly synopsis of laser construction and operation.

J.P. Talbot, "Lasers in the Movies Reality Check: Science vs. Science Fiction," *Laser Stars,* accessed December 5, 2001. http://home. achilles.net. An informative examination of frequent misconceptions about lasers due to their often inaccurate depiction in science fiction films.

John A. Tirpack, "Military Lasers High and Low," *Air Force Magazine,* September 1999. www.afa.org. A clearly written overview of proposed airborne laser weapons.

David Voss, "Upstream: Silicon Lasers," *Technology Review,* June 2001. www.techreview.com. Talks about new uses of lasers in silicon chip technology for computers and other devices.

David R. Whitehouse, "Understanding CO2 Lasers," Raytheon Advanced Laser Development Center, accessed November 27, 2001. www.laserk.com. A fairly detailed summary of the CO2 laser and its operation.

Index

Picture Credits

Cover photo: © Bob Krist/CORBIS

© Bettmann/CORBIS, 12, 20, 27, 50, 53

© Jonathan Blair/CORBIS, 34

© Crown Copyright/Health & Safety Laboratory/Photo
   Researchers, Inc., 41

© Digital image © 1996 CORBIS; Original image courtesy of
   NASA/CORBIS, 29

© Hulton/Archive by Getty Images, 18, 36

Chris Jouan, 22, 25, 31, 32, 46, 49, 57, 59, 68, 78, 81, 92

© Ed Kashi/CORBIS, 39

Library of Congress, 15, 17

© NIH/Photo Researchers, Inc., 69

© Charles O'Rear/CORBIS, 75

© Antonia Reeve/Photo Researchers, Inc., 64

© Roger Ressmeyer/CORBIS, 60, 82, 89, 93, 95

© Dr. Rob Stepney/Aumer/Photo Researchers, Inc., 71

© Geoff Tompkinson/Photo Researchers, Inc., 66

About the Author

In addition to his acclaimed volumes on ancient civilizations, historian Don Nardo has published several books for young people examining important modern scientific discoveries and topics, among them *The Origin of Species: Darwin's Theory of Evolution; Germs; Atoms; The Extinction of the Dinosaurs;* and *Cloning.* Mr. Nardo lives with his wife Christine in Massachusetts.